Dreams of California

Nicol & Elliott

By

John T. Young

ISBN 979-8-88627-945-0 (print)
ISBN 979-8-88627-946-7 (ebook)

Subjects: Genealogy, Biography, California History

Cover photo by John T. Young

Frank Nicol and Jean Elliott, Wedding Day 1954

Dedication

This book is dedicated to Jean Elliott Nicol, who passed away in 2012 after a long struggle with Alzheimer's. Jean was a graduate of the University of California at Berkeley (Cal), where she was president of the student body and editor of *The Daily Californian* in 1944. After graduation, she worked at the Voice of America in New York. She married Frank Nicol in 1954 and raised three children: Susan, Todd, and Alan.

Over several decades, Jean developed a passion for genealogy and traveled to Scotland and Germany to study the Nicol family. From her home in Pauma Valley, California, she wrote scores of letters in search of the history of the Nicol and Elliott families. Her 1980 interview with Irene Hund Nicol, Frank's mother, produced invaluable insights into the Hund family and the history of San Francisco at the time of the 1906 earthquake.

While interviewing Irene, Jean explained why she was interested in genealogical research on the family:

"I think it's important for your children and your great-grandchildren to know how things were," she said. "That's the reason I'm interested in this, from an historical viewpoint. How did we all get where we are, and why? What kind of people were they? How hard did they have to work? What kinds of things did they have to go through to get where we are now?"

Table of Contents

Introduction

The marriage of Frank Nicol and Jean Elliott in California in 1954 united two families who left their homes centuries ago in Scotland and Ireland. Their ancestors endured perilous journeys in sailing ships across the Atlantic to America, where their descendants continued to migrate across the continent.

As the United States expanded its territory in the 19th century, more land and opportunity lured Americans westward. For many, the ultimate destination was California, a land rich in resources where the Nicol and Elliott families sought their dreams.

The Nicols arrived in New Orleans in 1844 and worked their way up the Mississippi River to Illinois before moving to California.

James George Nicol, Frank's great-grandfather from Scotland, was a coal miner who settled in Illinois before he joined the Gold Rush to California. After the gold fields played out he switched to farming, while his sons became attorneys.

Jean Elliott's second great-grandfather, Aaron, arrived in Pennsylvania from Ireland in the early 19th century and later settled in Ohio. Aaron and two subsequent generations of Elliotts were farmers in Carroll County, Ohio.

Raymond Elliott, Jean's father, arrived in Long Beach, California from Ohio in 1912. A graduate of the University of Chicago, he taught chemistry and coached football at Long Beach Polytechnic High School until 1916, when he attended the University of California at Berkeley (Cal). He received a master's degree in chemistry from Cal in 1918. Elliott subsequently moved back to southern California, where he joined Standard Oil before heading up his own companies, Oilfields Service Co. and Geoanalyzer Corporation in Long Beach.

While the focus of this book is on the Nicol and Elliott families, I have included several ancestral lines associated with them, including the Dodge, Rogers, Hund and Zech ancestors of Frank Nicol, and the Sherrill and Farr ancestors of Jean Elliott.

Although we are not defined by our ancestors, we owe them a great debt for their sacrifices and courage that have contributed to the heritage of this nation. Together, these families form a rich mosaic of American history.

It is my hope that this book may provide some answers to subsequent generations to the question posed by Jean Elliott Nicol: "How did we all get where we are, and why?"

1

Scotland to America

On 20 December 1844, James George McNicol and his wife Margaret arrived in New Orleans aboard the ship *Oakland*, accompanied by their infant daughter, Susan and his sisters Janet, Agnes, Alice, and Sarah. A five-year-old brother identified as Jeane McNicol was also listed on the immigration manifest.[1]

James was 19, Margaret 21. An immigrant from Scotland, he told New Orleans immigration authorities his occupation was farmer and his destination was Illinois. A description provided decades later by a California Voters list said James was "5-foot-9, fair complexion, blue eyes."[2]

The Times Picayune, a daily newspaper in New Orleans, said the weather was fair on that day and "twenty-three square-rigged vessels and ten steamers arrived here yesterday."[3]

James and his family disembarked from the *Oakland* on early Friday morning into a bustling city, the third largest in

America with a population of 102,000.[4] The McNicols arrived in good weather and just missed an outbreak of yellow fever which had raged through New Orleans, according to *The Times Picayune.*

It was surely an overwhelming experience for the 19-year-old immigrant from Scotland. Where to find lodging for himself, his wife and infant daughter, along with four sisters and a younger brother? Where should he look for work? Should he stay for a time in New Orleans, or head up the river to his stated destination of Illinois?

Regardless of the challenges posed by their arrival in New Orleans, it would have been a great relief to be on solid ground again.

The *Oakland* was a packet ship, one of many vessels that carried cargo, mail, and people. It departed Liverpool about six weeks earlier. Most passengers traveled in the steerage compartments, below decks.

Conditions varied from ship to ship, but the steerage section was normally crowded and damp. According to a Smithsonian Natural History Museum website, "limited sanitation and stormy seas often combined to make it dirty and foul-smelling. Rats, insects and disease were common problems."[5]

Over nine million immigrants sailed from Liverpool for America between 1830 and 1930, according to the National Museum of Liverpool. The port of New Orleans was popular because it had well-established transatlantic links based on the import of cotton and timber.[6]

University of New Orleans history professor Joseph Logsdon wrote, "An estimated 550,000 immigrants passed through the Port of New Orleans between 1820 and 1860, making it the second leading port of entry in the United States by 1837. In fact throughout the antebellum period," he continued, "New Orleans drew more immigrants than the ports of Boston, Philadelphia, or Baltimore."[7]

McNicol was a native of Kilbarchan, Renfrew County, a village in the west central lowlands of Scotland, known for its weaving industry. Located about fifteen miles west of Glasgow, Kilbarchan's current population is about 3,500. In 1831, its population was 2,141.[8]

Scottish historian William Metcalfe said the weaving industry in Renfrew County "has been carried on, like that of farming, from time immemorial. From a very remote antiquity, spinning was an almost daily occupation of the women. Every village had its weaver, and many of the farmers eked out their living by working at the loom."[9]

Was James McNicol a weaver, farmer, or both? On his immigration manifest, he listed his occupation as farmer. In the U.S. Census for Illinois in 1850 and California in 1860, he gave his occupation as miner. By the time the 1870 Census was taken in California, however, he said he was a farmer.

It is likely that McNicol, only 19, worked at whatever job was available after he arrived, because he had to support himself, his wife and child and several siblings.

His sisters, Janet, 29, Agnes, 24, Alice, 16, and Sarah, 9, apparently stayed in New Orleans or moved elsewhere, since subsequent U.S. Census records do not show them in McNicol's household.

In the 1860 U.S. Census, Alice McNicol is shown married to Robert Waugh of New Orleans. Janet, Agnes and Sarah were likely married, but marriage records from that time are scarce. And, they may have moved elsewhere before marriage.

Alice and Robert Waugh had six children, according to the 1870 U.S. Census, which lists the family in New Orleans Ward

10. In the 1860 U.S. Census, Alice listed her age as 29—the same age as her husband, Robert.[10] In the 1870 U.S. Census, however, she gave her age as 36, and as 50 in the 1880 U.S. Census.

Several records note her birth year as 1827, so she would have been 33 in 1860—not 29. It is possible that the census taker made a mistake when listing her age; however, it seems likely that Alice did not tell Robert Waugh her true age because women in the 19th century had limited options to work. Marriage was viewed as desirable, especially for an immigrant woman who may have struggled to survive in a new world.

She may have decided that telling her future husband that she was four years older was a risk not worth taking. Alice and Robert were likely married in 1851, since their first child, Elizabeth, was born in 1852. It is unknown how Alice made a living from her arrival in 1844 to that time, but the prevalence of weaving in Kilbarchin suggests it's likely she was a dressmaker or weaver.

Alice died on 27 April 1902 in New Orleans, at age 75; the death record put her year of birth at 1827.[11] Her husband, Robert, died in Colon, Cuba in 1877, at age 46. A Presbyterian church record in New Orleans shows he died of "congestion of the brain." [12]

Yellow fever was widespread in Cuba in the late 19th century, so Waugh's death may have resulted from that disease.

He was buried in New Orleans, so he was likely on a business trip to Cuba. Waugh, a native of England, was naturalized as a U.S. citizen in 1853. He arrived in New York in 1849 and subsequently moved to New Orleans. Several city directory listings in the 1870s list him as an engineer.

No records were found to indicate what James McNicol did for a living or where he lived from 1844 to 1848, but New Orleans at that time had a thriving economy, and laborers were in demand for construction of canals and an expanding city.

Some relatives of the Nicol family recount stories that McNicol was a teacher, and that he taught school in New Orleans. No records could be located to verify that account, which is unlikely given his age and subsequent occupations.

Another family legend maintains that Margaret Lyle McNicol was the daughter of the Duke of Argyll, and that she was disinherited by her father after she married McNicol, a commoner.

That story is unlikely since the 7th Duke of Argyll, John Campbell, married Sarah Cunningham and later Joan Glassel. He did not have any relatives named Lyle. The 8th Duke of Argyll, George Campbell, also has no connection to Margaret Lyle. The Campbells lived in the late 18th and early 19th centuries.

There is a Margaret Lyle who married Matthew Stewart, the 2nd Earl of Lennox; however, she was born in 1465, according to *The Peerage of Scotland* historical accounts.

On the day the McNicol family arrived, *The Times Picayune* noted the arrival of the *Oakland.* The front page also advertised a slave auction that day, and several rewards were posted for runaway slaves.

The McNicol family arrived at a time when America was embroiled in controversy over slavery. An article in *The Times-Picayune* published on the day of their arrival, entitled "Foreign Impertinence," denounced "English fanatics" and members of the Free Church of Glasgow for criticizing the hanging of abolitionist John Brown.[13]

The Picayune Book Bindery advertised its treatment for the common cold: "Wright's Indian Vegetable Pills." In addition to curing the cold, the pills would cause the digestive system to be improved and "the blood so completely purified that all evil consequences from catching cold will be entirely prevented."[14]

Port of New Orleans by Alfred Waud
(Image courtesy of Alamy, Inc.)

When the McNicols moved north to Missouri and Illinois, they likely traveled by steamboat. Beginning in the early 1800s, steamboats enabled travel upstream from New Orleans through the lower Mississippi River Valley. The steamboats brought produce from the interior to New Orleans for export and return trips northward carried many of the immigrants from Europe.

In the 19th century, New Orleans was the largest port and most important city in the South, exporting most of the nation's cotton output and other products to Western Europe and New England. Steamboats made trade along the Mississippi much faster, and as a result, New Orleans thrived. By 1840 it was the second-largest port in America, after New York.

The 20 December 1844 edition of *The Times-Picayune* advertised passage for both sailing ships and steamboats. Two sailing ships were bound for Liverpool, one for Havana, and others for New York, Philadelphia, and Galveston. The steamboats offered passage to Ohio, Alabama, St. Louis, and other U.S. destinations.

The earliest record found of James George McNicol outside of New Orleans appears in the *1848 Passengers and Immigration List, 1500s-1900*, which records him applying for U.S. citizenship in St. Louis, Missouri.[15]

According to the California Voters Registration List, 1866-1896, Nicol was naturalized as a U.S. citizen in October 1850 in the Missouri Circuit Court.[16]

Other records show he lived in Missouri in 1849. His daughter, Alice, was born in July 1849 in Missouri, according to the 1850 U.S. Census and later census records.[17]

Whether he lived in New Orleans from 1844 to 1848 or moved directly to Missouri is unknown.

The 1850 U.S. census lists James "Nichols," 25, living in Madison County, Illinois. His occupation: "collier" in the coal mining industry. Also on that census: Margaret, 26, daughters Susan, 6, and Alice, 1. His younger brother, Colin, 17, was also on the census.[18]

It is possible that immigration authorities changed the spelling of his last name for him—a practice not unusual for that time. He was now an American, and like many immigrants, he may have sought to Americanize his surname, which would become "Nicol" by the time he reached California.

The 1850 Census is the first known record of Colin McNicol—James's younger brother—living in the United States. Colin also lists his occupation as collier, one who works in a coal mine; as opposed to a "miner," who works in different mines. He was not listed as an immigrant on the 1844 immigration manifest in New Orleans.

It is likely that he arrived on the *Oakland* and his name was not recorded amid the chaos of passengers disembarking in the Port of New Orleans. Colin would have been only 11 when the family arrived in New Orleans.

Colin did not appear on a search of the National Archives for the arrival of immigrants from Scotland; however, those records are incomplete and depend heavily on the information provided by local authorities.

No other records were located regarding Jeane McNicol, age 5, who was listed on the 1844 manifest. Jeane would have been only 11 in the 1850 U.S. Census. It is possible that Jeane lived with one of his older sisters, Janet, Alice, or Agnes.

The Missouri Court Circuit where James George McNicol was naturalized was in St. Louis, which is just 26 miles south of Alton, Illinois, in Madison County. Alton was the main shipping port for Illinois on the Mississippi River in 1850, according to historian Wilbur Norton.

Based on subsequent records in California, it is likely that James and his family lived in or near Alton. On his arrival in New Orleans, he told immigration authorities that his destination was Illinois.

In 1848, Alton had a thriving economy, according to an article in the *Alton Telegraph and Review*: "The stores are generally well stocked with goods of every description, and thronged with customers—our streets are crowded with people or wagons, laden with produce, as to be almost impassable, and the greatest activity seems to prevail in every department of domestic industry."[19]

Coal mining was a major industry in Madison County in 1850, and Alton was a major river port for shipping coal. As early as 1836, Norton wrote, "Alton was considered the head of navigation for New Orleans boats and many of the upper river boats turned back up the river from Alton, and Ohio river boats came to Alton and turned back from there."[20]

As James McNicol and his family settled in America, political events were occurring that would ultimately affect their destiny and that of all subsequent generations of Nicols.

In the mid-19th century, America was embroiled in a conflict with Mexico over Texas and was still vying for lands in the western half of the continent, where Great Britain was competing for the rights to Oregon Territory.

When McNicol arrived in New Orleans on 20 December 1844, *The Times Picayune* printed a resolution by the state of Alabama, stating that "neither Mexico or England nor any other power has a right to complain if Texas be annexed to this Union" and also said that the title of the United States to Oregon Territory "is clear and indisputable."[21]

In 1845 the United States annexed the Republic of Texas and went to war with Mexico from 1846 to 1848 in a dispute over the southern border of Texas. The United States won the war and received the territories of New Mexico and California as part of the post-war settlement.

The U.S. victory over Mexico in early 1848 was followed only a few months later by the discovery of gold in the Sacramento Valley, which sparked the California Gold

Rush, one of the most significant events to shape American history.

When James and Colin Nicol moved to California in the early 1850s to search for gold, their experience in the coal miles of Illinois would have given them skills for that endeavor.

To reach California, the Nicols could travel overland across the plains, the Rocky Mountains and Sierra Nevada Mountains. Or, they could ride a steamboat to New Orleans and book passage to Panama, cross the isthmus and take a ship to San Francisco.

In a 1974 interview with Susan Nicol, Lawrence Nicol, the grandson of James, recalled his father Frank telling him about traveling west in a covered wagon.

"My father used to tell me about all the sights that he saw, the buffalo and all that, but it was all make believe because he wasn't old enough to remember any of that," Lawrence said. "He heard his father talking about those experiences. He thought he remembered it. He was there, but he was a small child, and he couldn't remember anything."[22]

James Nicol had moved to California to mine gold, but moved back to Alton following the deaths of two young sons in 1857. Nicol family accounts maintain that Margaret Lyle Nicol was distraught over the deaths of her two young sons and wanted to escape the hard life of a mining camp.

Frank D. Nicol was born on 17 February 1859 in Alton, Illinois, and the family moved back to California when he was about four months old. James's younger brother Colin had remained in California, and it is likely that he persuaded his brother to return.

No records could be found about their first trip. If they had traveled down the Mississippi River to New Orleans, they could have visited one sister, Alice, who married Robert Waugh.

At some point, Alice's father, Colin McNicol Sr., appears to have been living with the Waughs in New Orleans.

Colin was not listed on the 1850 U.S. Census or on the 1844 immigration records; however, he is found in the 1860 U.S. Census as living in St. Bernard, Louisiana, post office Bienvenu, located southeast of New Orleans. His occupation was "gardener" at age 68, living with his daughter, Alice Waugh, 29, and her husband, Robert Waugh, age 29, with four children.[23]

No other records were found on Colin after 1860, so it is likely he died in the St. Bernard Parish or in New Orleans. Since Colin was born in 1792, his age of 68 matches the 1860 census.

It's unknown when Colin emigrated to America, but a search of Scottish records revealed no records of Colin or his wife, Alice after 1841. Alice apparently died in Scotland. Colin may have come with his sons and daughters to America, but no immigration record was found for him.

Colin McNicol and Alice George were married on 24 September 1814 in Kilbarchan, Renfrew County, Scotland, according to the Old Parish Registers of Scotland.[24]

He was born to Archibald McNicol and Agnes Campbell., who were married on 25 March 1786 in Inveraray, Argyll, Scotland, according to Scottish marriage records.[25]

The arrival of the McNicol family in America in 1844 coincided with an economic downturn in Scotland and Ireland. In Argyll, many people left for America.

According to the *Encyclopedia Britannica*, the Potato Famine in the Scottish Highlands that began in the mid-1840s caused distress and encouraged landowners to engage in a new round of clearances of tenant farmers and to sponsor large-scale emigration.[26] Ireland was also devastated by the famine.

James George McNicol left Scotland with a long legacy. The Scots were a blend of Neolithic survivors mixed with Celtic Picts, Brittonic Celts, Celtic invaders from Ireland, Viking and Norse Raiders and settlers, and Norman and Flemish Knights.[27]

He was descended from people who were always on the move, searching for new lands. His search would end in California.

2

Tuolumne County

By 1851, James George Nicol had left his home in Alton, Illinois and moved to Tuolumne County, California. After his arrival in California, he identified himself as "Nicol." He settled in Pine Log, a village just a few miles outside the mining town of Columbia, located near Sonora, the county seat.

It's unknown just how the Nicols reached Tuolumne County, but the journey would have been difficult.

Based on an interview with his grandson, Lawrence Nicol, they likely made at least one trip across the country in a Conestoga wagon, a large, covered wagon used heavily in the 19th century by settlers headed west across America.

The journey into California gold country was often hazardous. If the Nicols crossed the Sierra Nevadas in a wagon, they could have traveled over Ebbetts Pass, a very steep road running about sixty-one miles from Markleeville in Alpine County to Arnold in Calaveras County. The pass, which is closed during the winter, reaches an elevation of 8,736 feet.

Another route, the Sonora Pass, runs from Bridgeport to Sonora and climbs up to 9,624 feet. It is also closed in the winter.

"The first roads into Tuolumne County were rough, narrow and dangerous. Bandits were constantly waylaying teamsters, express riders and stage drivers," wrote historian Edna Bryan Buckbee in her 1935 *The Saga of Old Tuolumne.*[1]

Gold was plentiful in Columbia, Buckbee wrote, but the roads were "just hill trails that had been broken by wild animals and even wilder Indians."[2]

The lure of gold attracted thousands of prospectors to the county, which was one of the most prosperous in the California mining belt. Buckbee said gold was first discovered in Columbia in March 1850. Within weeks, settlers arrived and began erecting tents and shanties, which soon gave way to buildings and streets. She said of Columbia in 1852:

"The town supported forty saloons and gambling halls, a long thoroughfare flanked on both sides by fandango and hurdy-gurdy houses, three theaters, including a Chinese playhouse with Chinese actors, and seventeen general mercantile stores."[3]

Columbia had its share of saloons, but it also offered a semblance of culture, according to Buckbee: "Columbia boasted the most outstanding brass band in California. All of the thirty-two musicians had been training in the leading conservatories of Europe. These talented players from Germany, Austria, England, Italy and France were organized into a band by Professor Harris in the early part of 1852."

Within a few years after the discovery of gold in Columbia, it was transformed from shanties and tents into a prosperous town with hotels, restaurants and mercantile stores. Wells Fargo also had an office in downtown Columbia.

In 1853, according to Buckbee, Wells Fargo ran a daily express to and from San Francisco, Stockton, Jamestown, Sonora and Columbia.

Wells Fargo Office, Columbia, 2021
(Photo by John T. Young)

The Sonora Union Democrat wrote in the summer of 1854: "Columbia is running ahead like a quarter horse. Life and activity are its chief traits. It contains many fine buildings, displaying a high order of taste. The streets are kept clean and cool. There are not many loafers and "dead heads" about the saloons."

Unfortunately for the citizens of Columbia, most of its buildings were made of wood and vulnerable to fire. In 1854, a fire ignited in the town and destroyed most of it.

Columbia was quickly rebuilt, with brick and stone replacing the clapboard wooden structures that burned down. The saloons took priority. Ferguson's Saloon, located at the corner of Main and Fulton streets, soon featured "Florentine mirrors extended from ceiling to floor with a mahogany bar resplendent with crystal," according to Buckbee.

Another fire swept through Columbia in 1857, the same year that tragedy struck the Nicol family. James G. Nicol Jr., age 5, and his brother, Colin, age 3, died on November 3rd after eating poisonous berries. They were buried in the Columbia cemetery.

The *U.S. Find A Grave Index*[4] shows that James G. Nicol Jr. was born in April 1852 in Tuolumne County, which indicates that the Nicol family arrived there before that date—likely in 1851, since winter travel would have been very difficult.

The citizens of Columbia again rebuilt the town after the fire, but for the Nicol family, the loss of two young sons apparently was devastating. The tragedy may have been the reason the family moved back to Alton, Illinois.

James and Margaret likely decided that a frontier mining town was not a good place to raise children. Earlier that year, a daughter, Sarah, was born in Columbia. Their first child, Susan, born in Scotland, was 13 and Alice, born in Missouri, was 8.

The date of their return to Illinois is unknown, but Frank David Nicol was born in Alton on 17 February 1859.[5]

**Nicol gravesite, Columbia Cemetery
(Photo by John T. Young)**

Colin Nicol, James's brother, was 26 and still living in Pine Log in 1859. He apparently convinced James that gold mining was still a lucrative venture, and the family moved back to California about four months after Frank was born.

Nicol may also have been concerned about the Civil War that was on the verge of erupting. An unsigned letter titled "Conflict of the Century" ran in the *Alton Weekly Courier* on the day Frank David Nicol was born: "The successful resistance of Illinois to the aggression of slavery will be marked as an epoch in the nation's annals."[6]

Illinois was a free state, but Missouri, just across the river, entered the Union in 1821 as a slave state following the Missouri Compromise of 1820.

Nicol, therefore, straddled two states that were divided over the issue of slavery. While his motivation to move to California may have been primarily due to the lure of gold, by moving back to California he avoided some of the intense political turmoil that would eventually lead to the Civil War in 1861.

After returning to California, the Nicol family settled in Gold Spring, another mining settlement near Pine Log and Columbia. Gold Spring was discovered at the end of March 1850 by E. Hatch, who found gold while dipping water from a spring.[7]

By the end of the year, still another tragedy struck the family. On Christmas Day, 1859 Colin Nicol was shot in downtown Columbia and died the next day. Patrick Flanigan was arrested and charged with murder.

On 6 January 1860 a Tuolumne County Grand Jury said Flanigan "willfully feloniously and of malice aforethought did shoot off and discharge from the pistol the leaden bullet therein contained against and into the said Colin McNicol, then and there inflicting upon the person of the said Colin McNicol one mortal wound." After the case was examined further, the charge was reduced to manslaughter.[8]

No details of events leading up to the shooting were in the records, but Columbia at that time was a Wild West mining town. Shootings and murders were not uncommon in a town with forty saloons. The possible accidental shooting of Colin was not without precedent.

In 1850, according to an article about Columbia in the *Stockton Times*, "Miles O'Connor drew a pistol to shoot a man who had insulted him, fired twice and killed two passersby."[9]

Nicol family accounts passed down through generations maintain that Colin was walking by a saloon when a gunfight broke out, and he was an unlucky victim. Since the charge against Flanigan was reduced from murder to manslaughter, that account seems plausible. The murder charge would have required evidence of intent by Flanigan to kill Colin.

Flanigan was sentenced to nine years in prison for shooting Colin Nicol.

A few years before Colin Nicol was shot, murders had become so prolific in Columbia that vigilante groups formed to hang suspects. According to historian Buckbee, the Tuolumne County grand jury issued a report calling on "all good citizens to abandon their vigilante activities."[10]

James Nicol remained in Gold Spring and apparently continued mining for gold. In the 1860 U.S. Census, he listed his occupation as miner. His address on the census form listed Township 2, Columbia Post Office,[11] but he actually resided in Gold Spring, where he eventually abandoned gold mining and became a farmer, raising pears and apples.

On 14 October 1864, Nicol purchased a parcel of land in Gold Springs from A. Lewis for $375.

The deed describes the property as "one hundred meters west of the public highway leading from Columbia to Gold Springs on the north by the land of King Ketley, on the east by land owned by P. McFlask and by land on the south owned by W.H. Rier and N. Soderer and by the water ditch or canal of the Tuolumne Water Company, containing twenty-five acres of ground."[12]

In a 1974 interview with Susan Nicol, Lawrence Nicol, the grandson of James, recalled visiting his grandfather in Columbia as a young boy. His grandmother, Margaret, died when he was four, so he doesn't remember her, but he recalled that his grandfather had "a sandy red beard."

"He was a miner. Then he got some horses and big wagons and took fruit that he grew, apples and pears, and went over the summit to the Comstock, where he sold them," Lawrence said.

"He got about a dollar apiece for each apple," he recalled. "I was a very small boy when I last saw him. And I remember seeing these wagons with great big high wheels."

On both the 1870 and 1880 U.S. Censuses, Nicol listed his occupation as farmer, with a Columbia Post Office. In the 1880 Census, his son Frank, 21, gave his occupation as lawyer and place of birth Illinois. His daughter Alice, 26, said her occupation was dressmaker.[13] Could Alice's occupation have been a legacy of the McNicol family in Scotland, where weaving was a major industry? And, it may have been a source of income for her aunt Alice in New Orleans.

Nicol's first daughter, Susan, who was born in Scotland in 1844 on the eve of the family's departure for America, married Daniel Johnson in Columbia in 1863, when she was 19. In 1866, the Johnsons named their second child Colin.

James George Nicol died on 6 June 1900, just days after he was recorded by the U.S. Census as living in Columbia, Tuolumne County. His daughter, Alice, 50, was still living with him. She died two days later, on June 8.

An obituary in *The Evening Mail* in Stockton said Nicol had been ill with malaria. "Miss Nicol was sick with the same disease, and the death of her father was so much of a shock to her that she was unable to bear up in her weak condition, and yesterday she also passed away."[14]

Alice never married and always lived with her parents.

Columbia Cemetery
(Photo by John T. Young)

Nicol's wife, Margaret, died on 27 November 1892. James and Margaret are buried in the Columbia cemetery, next to their sons, James G. Nicol, Jr, and Colin. Their daughter, Sarah, is also buried there. She died at age 17, likely from pneumonia.

Also buried in the family plot is Alice and James's brother Colin, who was shot to death in downtown Columbia.

3

Descendants of James Nicol

Deeper than the incidents of his being, scarcely recognized by himself, surged in his heart and veins the blood which has made his ancestral Scotland a land of moral heroisms.

- Judge E.I. Jones, eulogy to Frank David Nicol, 4 April 1910, Stockton, California.

Born on 17 February 1859 in Alton, Illinois to Scottish immigrants James George Nicol and Margaret Lyle, Frank David Nicol departed life in Stockton with a sterling reputation as an attorney.

As noted by Judge Jones, Nicol achieved his reputation through hard work and talent.

"Be it remembered," Jones said, "that this man came to us of Stockton without fortune or prestige, called as events proved, to large matters of law, citizenship and manhood."[1]

Nicol attended public school in Columbia, then moved to San Francisco to attend Heald's Business College. He planned a career in law, but law schools barely existed in California at that time.

The first law school was established in 1878 at the University of California Hastings, in San Francisco[2]. It was likely too expensive for a young man from Columbia.

After graduating from Heald's, Nicol returned to Columbia, where he "applied himself to law, studying in the office of E.R. Galvin in Sonora," according to the *Stockton Daily Evening Standard*.

The State Bar of California was organized on 29 July 1927. Prior to that time, according to the State Bar, attorneys were usually admitted to practice law after being examined by justices at one of the California District Courts of Appeals or the Supreme Court.

Nicol, like most aspiring attorneys, acquired his legal skills through his mentor, Attorney E.R. Gavin of Sonora.

He was admitted to the State Bar of California in 1880 and practiced in Sonora for eight years. In 1882, he was elected to the California House of Representatives for one term, as a Democrat. He moved to Stockton in 1885 and practiced law there for 21 years.

Nicol set up his legal practice with a partner, Melvin H. Orr, and later was joined by another attorney, William B. Nutter. Nicol became president of the First National Bank in Stockton and served on the boards of directors of Pacific Gas & Electric and the Stockton Library.

Frank David Nicol, circa 1890
(Photo from Nicol Archives)

In 1900, after U.S. Representative Marion Devries died, delegates to the Second Congressional District in San Joaquin County recommended that Nicol fill the vacancy.

"The Hon. Frank D. Nicol, who, by reason of his talents, ability, experience, learning and eloquence, is one of the best equipped men for public life in this state, and whose character is such as to merit the unlimited confidence of our people," the resolution stated.

Nicol, however, declined the honor, saying he was not a candidate for the office.[3]

**Frank David Nicol, circa 1900
(Photo from Nicol Archives)**

In an earlier article in *The Evening Mail*, a reporter interviewed Nicol after he returned from a fishing vacation in Oregon. Nicol had not been aware of his nomination for Congress. The reporter wrote that Nicol was "too much engrossed in the pleasures of outdoor life and in catching fish to bother with the affairs of the world."[4]

In his eulogy for Nicol, Judge Jones said, "He became eminently admirable and influential at every bar to which he was called by his many, various and important retainers. He was at home in any court, effective alike in civil and in criminal cases, before the Court or before the jury. He excelled in the examination of witnesses."[5]

In a memoriam to Nicol, which was framed and hangs in the guest house at Board's Crossing, Calaveras County Judge A.J. McSorley says, "Endowed with a philosophical mind and extensive reading in prose and poetry, guided by his fine literary taste, added to his keen sense of humor, made his addresses before Court and Jury, gems of literary art."

Throughout his career, McSorley said, Nicol "scorned every form of falsehood and deceit, and his word was never questioned or impeached."

McSorley went on to say that Nicol's early life in the mountains, hills, and rivers of Tuolumne County "made him a sincere lover of nature through his life, and his too infrequent vacations were spent in the mountains along the streams of our County"[6]

On 30 July 1881, Nicol married Adelaide Louise Dodge, who was born in Tuolumne County.[7] Adelaide was the daughter of Dr. Mark Tyler Dodge, who moved from New York to Columbia in 1854—just a few years after James George Nicol and his family arrived from Illinois.

Adelaide Dodge Nicol, circa 1894
(Photo from Nicol Archives)

Frank and Adelaide had four children: Edwin, 9 May 1884; Susan, 8 December 1885; Lawrence, 17 September 1888, and Helen, 30 June 1892.

According to his World War I draft registration card, Edwin Nicol lived in Queens, New York in 1918. He listed his occupation as "Real Estate" and was employed by Freehold Realty Company, 2296 7th Avenue, New York. He was described as tall, with a stout build, hazel eyes and black hair.[8]

A 27 November 1957 obituary in the *Oakland Tribune* said Edwin was a retired salesman who died in Alameda after residing there for 17 years. Edwin and his wife, Hazel Marshall Nicol, had six children.

A 1901 article in *The Evening Mail* in Stockton said Edwin had been chosen to read the Declaration of Independence at Stockton's Fourth of July celebration.

"He has been prominent among the high school debaters, has a good clear voice and will fill his part of the program well," the article said.[9]

Susan Alice Nicol married Robert Hays Smith in 1908. She turned to journalism in her middle life and became a columnist for the *San Francisco Examiner* in 1936.

A 1908 article in the *Stockton Evening Mail* announcing her engagement said Susan "has been a conspicuous figure in Stockton and San Francisco society the past few seasons. She is a charming girl who makes friends easily and has a host of them to wish her and her fiancé a happy future."[10]

According to an obituary in the *San Francisco Chronicle* on 3 January 1959, Susan "was in intimate of royalty and in her travels became the close friend of notable figures in industry and the arts all over the world."

"For close to a quarter of a century she chronicled the activities of the great and near-great in her column," the article said.[11]

Susan died on 2 January 1959 in Hillsborough, San Mateo County, California.

**Susan Nicol Smith and Jimmy Stewart, circa 1939
(Photo from Nicol Archives)**

Susan's sister, Helen Nicol, married Joseph Nielson, an Ensign in the U.S. Navy, on 5 March 1914. An article on their wedding in *The San Francisco Examiner* said that Nielson, assigned to the *USS Pittsburg*, had been delayed in reaching San

Francisco because "an imbroglio in Mexico prevented the young officer from leaving the *Pittsburgh*."[12]

Just a few months before the outbreak of World War I, the United States had its eye on Mexico, which was officially neutral during the war; however, Germany made several attempts to incite war between the United States and Mexico.

In early 1914, U.S. forces occupied Veracruz, the chief port on the east coast of Mexico, during the civil war of the Mexican Revolution. The action came after several unarmed American sailors from the *USS Dolphin* were arrested at the port of Tampico.

President Woodrow Wilson considered the regime of Mexican President Victoriano Huerto illegitimate, after learning that Mexico was about to accept weapons and munitions from Germany. The "Battle of Veracruz" was over by 24 March, with U.S. forces occupying Veracruz for six months.[13]

It's unclear what role Nielson played in the Mexico incident, but his descendants say he served in submarines in the Atlantic during WWI.

The *Examiner* article said Helen was "an extremely attractive and vivacious girl and a popular member of social sets on both sides of the bay. Her husband is the son of a well-known Idaho cattleman."

Nielson was a 1911 graduate of the U.S. Naval Academy. He would spend the next several decades in the U.S. Navy, serving on cruisers, battleships, and submarines.[14] He retired as a Lieutenant Commander in 1934, the same year he married Katherine Sanford in New London County, Connecticut.

It's unclear when he divorced Helen Nicol, but they are shown as a married couple in the 1930 U.S. Census. Helen and Joseph had three children: Joseph Leroy Jr., Susan, and Soffe.

Helen Nicol Nielson, circa 1914
(Photo from Nicol Archives)

Nielson was recalled to service after the outbreak of World War II. In the Naval Reserve Register of 1 January 1943, Nielson is listed as a full commander.[15] His WWII service ended in 1946. Nielson died in 1967 in California.

Nielson was the son of Niels P. Nielson, who was born in 1852 in Denmark.. He emigrated to America in 1868 and became a successful cattleman in Idaho.

His son, Joseph Leroy Jr., was a physician who built a home just upriver from the Nicol home at Board's Crossing.

Helen Nicol Nielson died in Alameda, California at age 64 from complications following "a major operation," according to an obituary in *The San Francisco Examiner* on 16 March 1957.[16]

Frank David Nicol's brother, George Woodburn Nicol, was born in Columbia in 1862. Like his older brother, George also became a lawyer in Sonora. For several years, he was a partner with Frank in his Sonora law firm.

George Woodburn Nicol, circa 1900
(Photo courtesy of Tuolumne Historical Society)

At age 27, George Nicol was elected as Superior Court Judge in Tuolumne County, a position he would hold for thirty years.

During an interview with Susan Nicol in 1974, Lawrence Nicol recalled his time with uncle George:

"He was a very good judge. He was so popular, he was a judge for more than thirty years," Nicol said. "He was a big Scotsman, with a red face. He'd swagger up and down the street. I was a small boy, but I recall everyone said, "Good morning, Judge.""[17]

In 1888, George married Julia Mock, who was born in 1859 in Sonora. She was the daughter of Abraham Mock, a Jewish merchant who emigrated from France to California, where he was naturalized in 1859.

Julia had a daughter, Harriet Clark, who was born in 1886 during a previous marriage. George and Julia did not have any children of their own.

In a 1922 obituary after Nicol's death, the *Stockton Daily Record* said he died at the Clift Hotel in San Francisco, after several months of care for treatment of kidney trouble. The article noted that George was the brother of Frank D. Nicol.

"The two noted lawyers were reared in Tuolumne County and were self-made men, whose schooling was in little red school houses in the hills. They both struggled through boyhood for education and won fame through hard work."

Judge Nicol was not an orator, as was his distinguished brother, the article said, "But he was a learned lawyer and his decisions were rarely overruled in appellate court."[18]

4

Lawrence Nicol

Lawrence Nicol was born in Stockton, California on 17 September 1888 to Frank D. Nicol and Adelaide Dodge Nicol. His parents had moved from Columbia to Stockton in 1885.

Stockton was a major depot for gold miners headed for the Sierra Nevadas. Located on the edge of a deep-water port at the head of the San Joaquin River, the city was founded in 1849 by Charles Weber and named after Robert Stockton, a U.S. Navy Commodore who helped capture California during the U.S. Mexican War. The Gold Rush began in California the same year Stockton was founded.

By the time Lawrence Nicol was born in 1888, Stockton had become a major hub for agriculture. The intersection of the San Joaquin and Sacramento rivers created a delta waterway system that enabled farmers to ship their produce to Sacramento and San Francisco.

The city was also becoming a hub for recreation. Two days before Lawrence was born, *The Evening Mail*, a Stockton newspaper, featured an ad for "The Sells Brothers Enormous United Shows," offering a "Real Roman Hippodrome and Three-Ring Circus."

The Evening Mail also ran an ad for "Buckley, Hatter and Tailor," which advised readers: "Don't Wear a Hand-Me-Down When Tailoring is So Cheap." The ad also advised: "Don't Buy a Hat at a Grocery."[1]

Lawrence Nicol, 1893
(Photo from Nicol Archives)

As Lawrence's father Frank established his law practice, the city grew in population and became more prosperous. In the

1900 U.S. Census, when Lawrence was 11, his family lived at 1045 Madison Street, in downtown Stockton. The city's population that year was 17,506.

Frank D. Nicol walked a few blocks to his law office. Horses, not automobiles, were the main form of transportation. The Nicol social life, Lawrence said, was centered around family activities.

"It was a more neighborly atmosphere then," he said during a 1974 interview with his granddaughter, Susan Nicol. "The home was a central gathering place. The family didn't need so much. There was a closer tie-in to the family units at that time. I thought it was a good thing."[2]

The Nicol home didn't have many luxuries. "We had no electricity," Lawrence said. "We had an old wood-burning stove, to heat the water for the bathtub on the stove."

As for groceries, "The milkman came around, took the milk out of a great big can, poured it in big pans, and we would skim the cream off these pans," he said. Meat deliveries were also made door-to-door in horse-drawn wagons.

"Then the bread man would come around in a wagon, every day, with four or five shelves in the back," Lawrence said. And the iceman "would come around with these huge chunks of ice. He had a scale and a big saw. The Chinese handled the vegetables. They had wicker baskets, one on each end of this long pole."

Radios first became available in the mid-twenties. "They were pretty complicated," Lawrence said. "Lots of dials. There were only one or two stations anyway. Up until that time, in the evening, usually people would take turns reading out loud."

Every family had a stable with at least one horse, Lawrence said. His family also had a donkey "for the children to ride."

The first automobiles arrived in Stockton in 1907, Lawrence said, "but they were so scarce, you could hardly see one." The city had a streetcar that was pulled by horses, and street sweepers to clean up after the horses."

When his parents moved from Sonora to Stockton, Lawrence said, his grandmother, Eliza Rogers Dodge, moved with them because his mother, Adelaide, was in poor health and unable to take care of the children by herself.

"Mother was more or less a semi-invalid as far back as I can remember," Lawrence said. "In many ways, my grandmother was more of a mother to me than my own mother. She was a brilliant woman."

Adelaide, Lawrence said, may have suffered from child birth complications and "was a victim of the ignorance of all those country doctors, who didn't know what they were talking about. Her medicine cabinet was always crowded with all kinds of pills and medicines."

His grandmother, Eliza, married Dr. Mark Tyler Dodge in Jamestown in 1855. Dodge, who moved to Jamestown from New York in 1854, died at age 34 in 1866 of unknown causes. During their time together, Lawrence said, Eliza assisted her husband and learned a great deal about his work as a doctor.

Lawrence said she "was one of a very small handful of women in that area. There were thousands of miners, but very few women. And he was the only doctor at that time. He had to do all kinds of work on patients under primitive conditions. He had to operate on the kitchen table. Suddenly he died, and she was alone."

Not long after he died, Lawrence said some Mexican miners came to her door around midnight, carrying an injured comrade. She opened the door, and the Mexicans came in, carrying the injured man.

"His leg was dangling," Lawrence said. "Crushed. She told them the doctor was dead, and to take him to the kitchen table. She cut his leg off, sewed him up and saved his life."

After her husband died in 1866, Lawrence said, Eliza found a job teaching school in Columbia.

"Grandma told me she used to ride horseback down from her home to teach school," Lawrence said. "There was a big old oak tree, with a hanging limb. On that trail, she saw some objects hanging there, and she approached and found that the vigilante committee had hung three desperados and they were swinging from that big limb.

"What these vigilantes did was for the benefit of the entire community," Lawrence said. "That reminds me of something happening right now. It was more effective than anything they are doing these days in San Francisco. Hanging would have a quicker effect than anything else."

In the 1974 interview with Susan, Nicol recalled that his father, Frank, traveled frequently. "He was an outstanding lawyer," Nicol said. "Several of the leading lawyers in San Francisco begged him to go in and work with them. Because he was a genius."

Following his father's career path, Lawrence enrolled at the University of California at Berkeley (Cal) and studied law. He was, however, a reluctant law student. "I wasn't too anxious to study law. My father wanted me to," he said.[3]

In the 1912 Berkeley yearbook, Nicol was listed as a senior in the Delta Chi fraternity, which was then an organization for law students.[4] He resided at 2509 College Avenue, Alameda, California and was registered as a Democrat, according to the California Voter Registration list.[5]

In the same year, Nicol was one of eleven students at the University of California who were granted membership in the

John Marshall Law Club, an organization in which members obtained practice in court procedures.

"Membership in the club is accounted a student honor," according to an article about Nicol in *The Evening Mail*, a Stockton newspaper.[6]

On 13 May 1914, Nicol received his law degree from the University of California, according to *The Evening Mail*.

He apparently didn't waste any time going to work. On the 14 May 1914 roll of California Occupational Licenses,[7] Nicol is listed as an attorney in Mill Valley, a city in Marin County located about 14 miles north of San Francisco.

Only a month later, on 18 June 1914, the Archduke Franz Ferdinand—heir to the Austrian-Hungarian empire—was assassinated in Sarajevo, Bosnia. Within a week, Russia, Belgium, France, Great Britain and Serbia had lined up against Austria-Hungary and Germany. World War 1 had begun.

The assassination of Archduke Ferdinand would ultimately change Lawrence Nicol's life.

On 2 April 1917, President Woodrow Wilson asked Congress to declare war against Germany, whose U-boats had been sinking U.S. merchant ships bound for Europe.

A few months later, on 5 June 1917, Lawrence Nicol registered for the draft, at age 28. He gave his home address as 2300 Van Ness, San Francisco and listed his occupation as attorney-at-law. He said he worked at the law firm of Goodfellow, Ells, Moore & Orrick at 433 California St., San Francisco.

**World War I recruiting poster
(Courtesy of the Smithsonian Institution)**

Nicol stated on his registration form that he had prior military service in the California infantry for two years.[8] His service was with the 16th Provisional Training Regiment at San Francisco, with the rank of corporal.[9] His service was likely with a unit of the California National Guard. The registrar said he was tall, with a medium build, gray eyes and dark brown hair.

Nicol's Army discharge record said that he was 5-foot-9 and a half inch tall when released from active duty on 22 July 1919.

The record said that he was inducted into the U.S. Army on 13 December 1917 in San Francisco.

After entering the Army, Nicol was sent to training camps at the Presidio, a fort on the Monterey Peninsula, and then to American Lake, a site near Tacoma, Washington next to Camp Lewis. His last duty station in the U.S. before going overseas was at Camp Lewis.

An article about Nicol and Camp Lewis in the *Stockton Daily Evening Record* on 28 January 1918 said Nicol "writes Stockton friends that he is enjoying the life there and like all the other boys hopes to be ordered into foreign service soon."[10]

World War I marks the first time that the United States sent soldiers abroad to defend foreign soil. When the United States declared war against Germany, the nation had a standing army of 127,500 soldiers. By the end of the war, four million men had served in the U.S. Army, with 800,000 in other branches of service.

During the war, the United States sustained more than 320,000 casualties, with 53,000 killed in action. Another 43,000 soldiers died mainly due to the influenza pandemic of 1918.[11] An estimated 675,000 American civilians died from the flu in 1918.

On 16 March 1918, Nicol shipped out from New York, headed for France. According to the U.S. Army Transport Service, he was with the Third Replacement Company from Camp Lewis.[12]

On arriving in France, Lawrence Nicol was an infantry soldier, but when he returned on 13 July 1919, he was with the 1st Censor & Press Company, which was an element of a newly formed Army intelligence unit."[13]

**Lawrence Nicol, circa 1919
(Photo from Nicol Archives)**

According to James L. Gilbert, author of *World War I and the origins of U.S. Military Intelligence*, the American Expeditionary Force in Europe created an intelligence system based on the British model in August 1917. The system included a "Censorship" division. The Army decided to transfer soldiers "who were proficient in foreign languages,"[14] to the new division.

How did Nicol go from the infantry to intelligence? According to his wife, Irene Hund Nicol, the move was due to an opportune encounter with her brother, Walter Hund.

"Papa (Lawrence) and I met because he and Wallie met in France during World War I, one dark night in front of the Chateau in St. Anyan," Irene said during a 1980 interview with Jean Elliott Nicol, her daughter-in-law. "They were the only Californians there—most of them were from the East."[15]

Nicol and Hund formed a friendship that led to Nicol joining Hund in his interrogation unit, according to a story passed down through several generations of the Nicol family.

Serving as an interrogator and not on the front lines as an infantry soldier may well have spared Nicol from death or injury on the battlefield.

Nicol's discharge record said that he had not been in any battles, engagements, or skirmishes. He received the Victory Medal for service in France and had an "excellent" character.

The friendship of Nicol and Wallie Hund continued after both men returned to California.

"When Lawrence came back, he came over to see Wallie. They had both been in the statistical division in the army and shared an apartment," Irene said. "Later, Wallie was transferred to the chemical warfare division because of his chemistry background."

Walter Hund deployed to France from New York on 11 Jan 1918 as a private in the 147th Field Artillery Regiment.[16]

After arriving in France, however, the Army discovered that Hund had skills it needed.

Hund was fluent in German, and the "statistical unit" to which Irene Hund referred was likely a euphemism for Army Intelligence.

"They were interrogators," Nicol's granddaughter, Susan Nicol Thibodeaux said during a 2020 interview. "That's what I heard. They needed German speaking people to do that. Now, to what extent Lawrence was fluent, I cannot say. My impression is, he had a rudimentary knowledge of German. Not like the Hunds did. Because the Hunds grew up speaking German. They learned German before they learned English."[17]

Susan and her brother, Todd Nicol, were told about Lawrence and Wallie being interrogators by their father, Frank Nicol. When Susan asked Lawrence about his Army service during a 1974 interview, he was reluctant to discuss his time in the Army. He provided very few details, beyond meeting his future brother-in-law, Wallie Hund.

During their service in France, Wallie showed Lawrence a picture of Irene "and promoted her," Todd said. "I think they started writing."

Later, Hund was assigned to the Chemical Warfare Laboratories in Paris as a research chemist, according to an obituary in the *Oakland Tribune*. He was a graduate student in organic chemistry at the Chemical Institute, University of Berlin, in 1910 and 1911.[18]

When Walter Hund returned to the United States in 1919, his rank was Sergeant Major in the Chemical Warfare Service. Lawrence remained in France for several months after the war ended and studied at the Sorbonne, in Paris. According to the *Stockton Daily Evening Record*, Nicol was attending college in France "to complete his mastery of the language."[19]

After he returned to California, Lawrence began to visit Wallie and Irene on weekends. "One day, Lawrence told me he had my picture," she said. "I asked him where he had gotten it. He said Wallie had left it on the mantle in their apartment in France, and he kept it."[20]

During his 1974 interview with Susan, Nicol said Wallie "made him promise when I got back to come to Ross to meet with the family. He came home before I did. I stayed and went to Sorbonne. When I got back, I rang him up, and that's when I met Irene."[21]

Irene also served during World War I. One of the few women in the UC-Berkeley (Cal) class of 1917, she also became one of the first women admitted to the U.S. Navy, serving as a yeoman. Irene graduated from Cal with a degree in entomology.

In 1987, Irene told a reporter from the *Contra Costa Times* that she worked in the Navy censor's office, checking all cables coming into San Francisco to see if any of the senders were on the "enemy list."[22]

Lawrence Nicol and Irene Hund were married on 20 Dec 1920 in Marin County, California.[23]

Before his marriage in late 1920, Nicol was an attorney living in San Francisco, according to the 1920 U.S. Census. He lived in Assembly District 31 and said he was self-employed.[24]

He soon decided to abandon his law practice and move to Brentwood, in Contra Costra County, a rural area about 55 miles east of San Francisco.

"I was going to stay out there for a year or two and get rich on the almond ranch," Lawrence said during his 1974 interview with Susan Nicol.

Lawrence said he learned about the almond ranch from a college friend who was a farm advisor in Contra Costa County. "He told me about a wonderful place out there that was a wonderful bargain. He took me out there and got me into it.," he said.

**Irene Hund Nicol, circa 1919
(Photo from Nicol Archives)**

Irene Hund Nicol, 1920
(Photo from Nicol Archives)

Despite his comments about getting rich and finding a great bargain on the almond ranch, Lawrence made it clear during the 1974 interview that he wasn't interested in practicing law.

"I didn't want to go into an office anymore," he said. "I never should have. I'm an outdoor man."[25]

Prior to his marriage, Nicol had bought the almond ranch in Brentwood, although Irene may not have realized that he was ready to leave the law profession and become a farmer. She likely thought the land was an investment, not a place to live. She would quickly face that reality.

An article in the *San Francisco Examiner* announcing their marriage said, "After a brief wedding trip the young couple will reside at Brentwood, Contra Costa County, where Mr. Nicol has extensive agricultural interests."[26]

"I heard that she thought she was marrying a sophisticated San Francisco attorney," said her granddaughter, Susan. "And then, all of a sudden, she's got to live in the middle of nowhere.

"She had three children relatively quickly. They were all in diapers at one point. She had no help on the ranch. She was exhausted," Susan said.

In his 1974 interview, Lawrence acknowledged the hardships that came with farm life in the 1920s. "It was a hard life out there. In 1920, the farmers were the first people to suffer from the effects of the Depression. From 1920 to 1930, agriculture was just going from bad to worse."

"In spite of all that," he said, "you got plenty of outdoor exercise and it kept you in good physical shape. You have some intangible gains you don't realize when you're going through those hard times."

Frank, Walter, Jean Nicol, 1925
(Photo from Nicol Archives)

Lawrence recalled one hot summer day on the almond ranch when he was visited by his father-in-law, Dr. Frederick Hund, who lived in Freestone.

"I was complaining about the heat and the hard work, and the summer was terrifically hot," he said. "He told me, you don't realize, that's going to extend your life. He says, you'll live ten years longer on account of that. It turned out just that way. My sisters and brother were sedentary. They didn't like to exercise. I think that's why they died sooner than I did."

Lawrence said his almond ranch was not sufficient to sustain his family in food because he was growing specialty crops, in an irrigation district.

"In the old days, you would grow everything to sustain yourself," he said. "You had sheep for wool, you had your chickens, you had your cows. But they created these irrigation districts. They would have all apricots, or all peaches, or all almonds."

During the Great Depression, he recalled, "I remember a farmer across the way had a beautiful peach orchard. After the Depression got so bad, he couldn't even hire the labor to pick his peaches, and they all fell on the ground. You would see a great golden circle of peaches under every tree."

Some aspects of life on the almond ranch were similar to Lawrence's earlier life in Stockton. The ice man still delivered blocks of ice, and a meat wagon came by the ranch.

"In the country, those things continued for a longer period of time," he said, "because you would only go to the store once a week. And you charged everything in the store. You paid the grocery when the crops came in. That made it very difficult when the crops didn't come in."

Lawrence recalled one year when he shipped 100,000 crates of honeydew melons "and ended up with nothing. They all sold, but the amount of money I made was only equal to the cost of raising them."

Winters were difficult because a wood-burning stove was their only source of heat. "It was fine in the winter because you kept it burning all the time," he said. "Everyone sat in the kitchen in the winter because it was the only warm room."

Lawrence and Irene continued to live on their almond ranch until their children graduated from Liberty Union High School in Brentwood. All of them attended the University of

California at Berkeley (Cal), which may have been a factor in Nicol's decision to sell their ranch and move to Berkeley after their youngest son, Walter, graduated from high school.

Frank, Jean, and Walter Nicol, 1941
(Photo from Nicol Archives)

It would have been difficult for Lawrence to manage the ranch alone at age 51. The 1940 U.S. Census shows Lawrence and Irene still living at Brentwood in Contra Costa County, with Frank, 18, Jean, 17, and Walter 16. The census record lists him as an orchard grower.[27] In 1941, he sold the ranch and moved to Berkeley.

Lawrence said his decision to sell the ranch came at the end of two decades of financial struggles. During the Great Depression, he said, "We had to sell half the ranch. We couldn't sell the crops. The farmers were in a terrible condition. That was in 1929, after the crash."

He said he originally had 600 acres. "We lost half of that. We had to move to this other house across the way, on the other 300 acres."[28]

Frank Nicol told his daughter, Susan that Lawrence owned the ranch with a partner, Robert Hays Smith, who was his brother-in-law.

Smith was a wealthy San Francisco businessman who suffered financially after the 1929 crash of the stock market and the resulting Great Depression.

"Uncle Bob (Smith) hadn't kept up his payments," Nicol said. "He couldn't pay anybody anything. He had property everywhere, and he couldn't do anything with the property. He couldn't even give it away."

Consequently, Nicol said, financial conditions made it necessary for his father to sell the ranch. "I think my father just gave over the ranch to them, but got eighty acres free and clear. Which he then sold."[29]

Lawrence and Irene subsequently moved to Berkeley, where he bought an apartment house next to the Grand Hotel.

"That was a good move," Lawrence told Susan during the 1974 interview. "Doubled my money. Everything I bought down there paid out."

After World War II began, Irene worked on the draft board, while Lawrence was employed from 1942 to 1945 as a production engineer. "I was making parts for Liberty ships. Machinist work. Helping the war," he said.

On 30 June 1942, Lawrence and Irene's youngest child, Walter registered for the draft. He had turned 18 on 9 April 1942. On his registration card, he gave his address as 2336 Piedmont Ave., Berkeley, the home his parents had bought after leaving Brentwood. He was 5-foot-9, 155 pounds, with blonde hair and blue eyes.[30]

On his draft card, Nicol said he was employed by Standard Oil. His son, Garrett (Garry) Nicol, said Walter attended Berkeley for one or two years before he was drafted in 1944 and sent to Europe as part of an armored division.[31]

After basic training, Walter was sent to an officer training school in Indiana.

"He thought it was an officer training program," Garry said. "And then the Army said, forget this, we need bodies in tanks, and sent them to Kentucky, where they did some really quick training, which they felt was inadequate. They put them with tanks on ships and off they went to Europe."

Garry said his father arrived in Europe at the end of 1944. His armored unit, the 20th Division, was mainly engaged in mopping up operations, as the Germans retreated from France back into Germany. Walter Nicol also saw some German concentration camps.

"The big thing was, he helped liberate Dachau," Garry said. "When we were growing up, there were photos of bodies at Dachau. Boxcars of bodies. All of us kids looked at them, and then eventually, he took them away and burned them."

Dachau, the first Nazi concentration camp, opened in 1933. Located in southern Germany near Munich, it was initially a camp for political prisoners but evolved into a death camp, where countless thousands of Jews died.

Walter Nicol was among the American soldiers who liberated Dachau on 29 April 1945. They found thousands of emaciated prisoners and several dozen train cars loaded with rotting corpses.

Walter also related a more pleasant memory from another part of Germany: "He said they met up with the Russians and had a big party," Garry recalled. "He would describe the Americans dancing with great big Russian women soldiers. And I think he did, too."

When Walter returned home to Berkeley, "Nobody came to meet him at the Alameda train station, because his father had put his car up on blocks because of the gas rationing, so he had to walk from the train station out to the family house in Berkeley. He walked across town with his duffel bag," Garry said.

In 1945, Walter married Mona Elaine Garrett, whom he met during his brief stint in officer training in Indiana. After Garry was born in 1948, they had three other children: Nancy, David, and Muriel.

Walter returned to the University of California at Berkeley (Cal) and earned a B.A. in entomology. After working as a mosquito abatement specialist for Ortho—a division of Standard Oil—he earned a teaching credential and taught handicapped students at a farm school at Cabrillo, California.

Walter's brother, Frank, graduated from Berkeley on 6 June 1943 and joined the U.S. Navy, where he was commissioned as an officer. Nicol served in the Pacific in 1945 as a torpedo officer on the U.S.S. McKean, which cleared Allied floating mines from Japanese waters after the surrender of Japanese forces.

Jean Helen Nicol was listed in the 1944 Berkeley yearbook as a senior. An article in the 12 May 1943 edition of the *Oakland Tribune* said she was engaged to Patrick Masterson, a senior at Berkeley.[32]

After they were married, Jean and Patrick had two daughters, Kathryn and Carolyn. Patrick died in 1968 and Jean married William Saylor in 1971.

"Auntie Jean was a real character," Garry said. "She loved to smoke and drink and tell stories."

**Walter, Irene, Lawrence, Jean, Frank Nicol, 1941
(Photo from Nicol Archives)**

After World War II, the Nicol home on Piedmont Avenue became a boarding house for female students attending Berkeley in the 1950s and 1960s.

"I can remember them running around in their towels," said Todd Nicol, recalling a visit to his grandparents in 1963, when he was 6. "And that's also where I was when John Kennedy died."

Asked to describe his relationship with Lawrence, Todd said, "He was a dude all to himself. He was not really communicative."

Susan agreed: "To say we were close is not accurate," she said. As for Irene, "She was a lot more fun."[33]

Susan also recalled the Piedmont House: "Because all these coeds lived there, and they would move out at the end of the school year, they would leave random things behind. Nothing of particular value."

Irene would take those random items to her parents' home in Freestone, located north of San Francisco in Sonoma County. Susan recalled that the items the girls left behind would often end up as prizes in a game played by the Nicol children.

"One of the things we used to do at Freestone, with Elaine and Walter's children, they had this little thing they got in Chinatown, where you poked a little thing through and a paper came out and you had to do what it said, like do a headstand, or sing happy birthday, or whatever.

"Then, if you successfully did it, you got to pick from the no-touch box. There was this box, with all the things the girls left, and you got to pick something. They were just little things that had been left. It was great fun," she said.

Garry Nicol also recalled the games: "You had to stand on one foot and tap your stomach and your head at the same time. Funny things like that. Whistle a tune."

Garry has good memories of his grandparents and Freestone, where he now resides with his wife, Marjorie. Nestled in a valley a few miles from the tiny village of Freestone, the Hund home was built on a hillside, surrounded by oak, pine and redwood trees. Irene's parents, Frederick Hund and Carrie Zech Hund bought the property and built the house about 1912. Frederick and Carrie both died in 1941.

Hund-Nicol home in Freestone, 2021
(Photo by John T. Young)

Irene and Lawrence Nicol were frequent visitors at Freestone and spent time there with their grandchildren.

"They made a huge impression on all of us," Garry said. "They were fabulously entertaining. Growing up, it was about as much fun as you could have, hanging out with them. Grandpa was a little gruff, but fascinating."

"Grandpa would rant and rave more. About politics. Maybe family members," Garry said. "I remember going into his bedroom here and seeing his false teeth up on the table. And he would wear a nightgown. In his dresser, he had a pistol from World War I in there.

"He had Roman coins, and some gold pieces," Garry said. "He would put sugar on his tomatoes and salt on his watermelon."

The Freestone property remains a gathering place for the Nicol family. It has been the scene of several weddings and numerous family picnics, which are held on a long table under towering pine trees just outside of the home.

Nicol family, Freestone, CA, 2013
(Photo by John T. Young)

Alan Nicol, Freestone, 2013

Todd Nicol, Murphy, Freestone, 2013
(Photos by John T. Young)

**Elaine and Walter Nicol, Freestone, 2013
(Photo by John T. Young)**

After they left Berkeley and the Piedmont house, Lawrence and Irene Nicol moved to Rossmoor in Walnut Creek, where they retired. They both died in Walnut Creek, which is about 30 miles west of Brentwood, where they had their almond ranch.

5

Frederick Hund, Jacob Zech

Frederick John Hund, Irene Nicol's father, was born in Homberg, Hessen-Kassel, Germany in 1858. His father, Heinrich Hund, died in Homberg in 1864 of unknown causes. Frederick was only 6 years of age.

According to an article in *The Bay of San Francisco: the Metropolis of the Pacific Coast, a history*, Heinrich "was a teacher in the seminary for the education of teachers" in Homberg.[1]

Very few details are available on Frederick or his parents in Germany, but Frederick arrived in New York on the ship *Danae* on 24 May 1872, at age 14.[2]

Frederick followed his brother, Otto, to New York and was later joined by his mother, Sophia and his sister, Marie. The Hund family left Germany during a turbulent time. A coalition of German states led by Prussia defeated France during the Franco-Prussian War, which began in 1870 and ended in 1871.

The war ended French hegemony in Europe and resulted in the creation of a unified Germany under Chancellor Otto von Bismarck. The war was followed by a depression, and Bismarck ruled in an authoritarian manner.

The Hunds, like thousands of other Germans, likely fled the country to escape the political and social unrest that followed the war.

**Sophia Frederick Hund: Frederick, Otto, Marie
(Photo from Nicol Archives)**

Sophia arrived in New York with her daughter, Marie, 12, on 29 May 1874 on the ship *Main*, which departed from Bremen, Germany.[3]

Marie attended public schools in New York City and married Charles Hartung on 24 Jan 1878, when she was 16.[4] Hartung, also born in Germany, was 38. He was a pioneer importer of human hair who owned a 300-acre estate near Wyckoff, New Jersey. Marie died in Wyckoff at age 92, in 1954. She was survived by eleven children.

Sophia Hund died on 29 Oct 1896 in Franklin, New Jersey. According to her New Jersey Death record, she was born in Germany in 1828.[5]

After arriving in America, Frederick Hund lived with his uncle, Dr. John Frederick, who owned a drug store in New York City. He served as an apprentice apothecary with his uncle until he began studying medicine in 1874 at the University of New York.

He graduated in 1879 with a Doctor of Medicine degree and practiced medicine at College Point, Long Island, then worked at the Northwestern Dispensary of New York, according to an 1892 article in *The San Francisco Call.*[6]

Frederick became a naturalized U.S. citizen in February 1880, in New York. In 1882, he moved to San Francisco. Like the Nicol and Elliott immigrants, he sought opportunity in California.

The article in *The San Francisco Call* said Hund was "a scholarly and hard-working member of the medical profession." The article went on to say that Hund "is an incessant reader."[7]

The *Call* said Hund devoted most of his practice to surgery. It also included information about Frederick's brother, Otto, who was born in Homberg in 1857. Otto graduated from the University of New York in 1877 with a medical degree and was licensed as a physician in California in 1881, a year before Frederick moved to San Francisco.

The city was host to many German immigrants, and Hund soon found a bride from a German family. On 16 September 1884, Frederick J. Hund and Caroline (Carrie) Zech were married in San Francisco.

According to the California Voter Registration List in 1890, Frederick's office and residence were at 757 Folsom Street, San Francisco. He was 32.[8]

In the 1900 U.S. Census, the Hunds were living in San Anselmo, Marin County, San Francisco. They had five sons: William, 16, Harry, 14, Fred, 13, Walter, 11, and Ervin, 10. Their only daughter, Irene, was 4.

The Hunds also had a housekeeper, Meta Seffene, 22, who was born in Germany, and a "coachman," Ambrose Regalia, 24, who was born in Italy. A nephew, William Grass, 15, also lived with them.[9]

Until 18 April 1906, Frederick Hund commuted into San Francisco, to his office on Folsom Street. That morning at 5:12 a.m., a massive earthquake broke loose in the city. It lasted less than a minute but destroyed nearly 500 city blocks and ignited fires that burned for three days.

The earthquake killed an estimated 3,000 people and left half the city's 400,000 residents homeless, according to the Center for Legislative Archives.[10] The quake was caused by a slip of the San Andreas Fault.

Frederick Hund was in Marin County when the earthquake erupted, but his office in downtown San Francisco was destroyed, along with 30,000 other buildings.

"Our whole life was blasted by the earthquake," Irene Hund Nicol said during a 1980 interview with Jean Elliott Nicol.[11]

Irene recalled sleeping with her cousin, Selma Berndt, "when all the stuff fell over our bed. I remember Papa saying, come here and stand under the doors.

"My brother Fred came flying down. He had had a hemorrhage before then and was supposed to be absolutely quiet in bed. You could hear him screaming down the stairs. My whole bed was full of dishes, because I had this cabinet next to the bed, with all kinds of lovely dishes.

"Before the earthquake my father had been practicing in San Francisco and commuted back and forth on the ferry," she said. "In San Francisco he had a buggy and a driver that took him around to make his calls."

Irene said her father "was an excellent doctor. He was one of the first ones to do some of the very serious surgery taking out a part of a person's stomach and hooking it together again, instead of just letting him die. He did a lot of work along those lines. He was on the diagnostic staff at St. Luke's Hospital in San Francisco for a long time. He was very particular about antiseptic practices in surgery, and studied and read constantly.

"Everything was very lovely and very prosperous before the earthquake," Irene said. "Then the earthquake came and just pulled the rug out from everything."

Irene, who was 10 in 1906, said her father lost valuable downtown property as a result of the earthquake. "In those days, people didn't invest in stocks and bonds. If you had some extra money to invest, it was always real estate," she said.

"We had nine properties south of Market. The earthquake knocked them all down and burned them all up," she said.

"And no insurance. My father's medical instruments were all burned up, his books, everything."

Irene recalled sitting out in a grove near her home at night with her father after the earthquake. "He said, It's all gone, everything we have is gone. The city's doomed. But if the boys get home, everything will be all right."

Two of Irene's brothers, Walter and Erwin, were at college in Berkeley. Later that night, they caught a launch to Sausalito and made it home.

Irene said her father had to start all over again, with an office in San Rafael. "He had all these boys who were college age. I don't know how he did it," she said. In 1909, he sent Walter and Fred to Germany for graduate work in chemistry, while Harry and Erwin went to Philadelphia to finish their medical studies.

A year after the earthquake, she said her father bought their first car, a Maxwell. "I drove a car when I was about 11. I'd just drive around Ross," she said. "They used to have signs that said, 'automobiles prohibited.'

"Of course, we always had horses. They used to take us down to the train in Ross. It was about a mile. The gardener was also the driver, and he took care of the horses, too," she said.

In the years before the 1906 earthquake, Irene said the Hund family would take camping trips during the summer. She recalled a trip to an area near Fort Bragg, a city on California's Mendocino Coast.

"There was a little stream, but no one had bathing suits," she said. "I was only six years old, so I put on a pair of pants. And Papa got gunny sacks and cut the corners out for the boys."

Two years later, she said, the family traveled to an old ranch on the Gualala River, located about 100 miles north of San Rafael, near Route 1. The area is now the site of the Gualala River Redwood Park and several campgrounds.

"We went swimming there," she said. I remember riding a horse bareback, without a saddle or bridle or anything. The horse would swim across the river, with me on it."

The Hund residence in Ross was on Laurel Grove Avenue. "Laurel Grove Avenue was a beautiful place," Irene recalled. "A wonderful climate. The house had three floors. The middle floor was the company floor, with living and dining room, Papa's library, what had been a music room but was turned into a billiard room. The bottom floor was the everyday floor. Upstairs were the bedrooms."[12]

After the earthquake, Hund purchased five acres contiguous to his home and built a sanitarium, El Recreo, or place of relaxation.

The sanitarium provided for twenty-five patients and included a laboratory for pathological and chemical research. With the advent of the automobile in Marin, Dr. Hund began receiving patients who had road accidents. He did emergency surgery for the victims.[13]

When she was 9, Irene went to a girl's school because "I didn't know how to play with girls," she said. "I grieved and said if I couldn't play with the boys, couldn't I sit on the fence and watch them?"[14]

Despite her misgivings, Irene learned to play with girls and made some good friends with girls at school. "We spent overnights and weekends at each other's homes," she said. "We all had horses, and wherever we were invited, our horses were invited, too."

When she was a teenager, her school had monthly dances with the two military academies in San Rafael. She had a party once before a dance. "It was when ragtime first came out. It was considered very daring."

Irene had the sheet music for a new song, "The Grizzly Bear," which someone put on the piano. "We thought we were very devilish," she said.

"Of course, we had chaperones," Irene said. "Your mother would go and sit there with you."

Irene grew up taking music lessons but, "I never liked the lessons and played things my own way."

She recalled her music teacher, Herr Widder, who "had this amazing talent for music." She did not get along well with him, she said, "because he always had unpleasant remarks about me being fat. And then he would show me how to play something, and I would play it back, but in another key. He would swear at me in German. He finally figured I wanted to play something with more zip to it."

Susan Nicol Thibodeaux, Irene's granddaughter, has a list of hundreds of Irene's favorite songs, which include "You Made Me Love You," "I Wonder Who's Kissing Her Now," "Down By the Old Mill Stream," and "Alexander's Ragtime Band."

About 1910, Irene said Frederick Hund bought property near Freestone, a rural area about 45 miles north of San Rafael, the county seat of Marin County.

"Wallie and Fred were in school in Germany, taking their post graduate work in chemistry, and they became interested in growing and manufacturing drugs," Irene said during her interview with Jean.

"They were looking for a place with lots of water, and that's when they found the acreage," she said. "The drugs they were interested in growing were digitalis, mint, and maybe belladonna."

Despite their chemistry background, Irene said, "They found they couldn't produce enough to make it pay."

Although the business venture failed, the Hunds decided that the Freestone property was a good place to build a house. Irene said the home was designed "from a drawing Wallie had made of a Swiss chalet he had seen in Europe."

After Frederick retired in 1921, the Hunds moved to their home in Freestone, several months after Irene and Lawrence Nicol were married.

Irene recalled the sale of the Hund home in Ross: "Our lovely home—sanitarium, laboratory, four housing units, a stable and garage plus six acres of gardens and seven acres of redwood grove and wooded hills sold to the Catholic Church for $35,000."

In 1928, the Hunds were involved in a serious car accident. According to an article in the *San Anselmo Herald,* their auto was stuck by a gravel truck after being crowded toward the left side of the road by another motorist.

Dr. Hund suffered minor cuts and bruises, but Carrie had a fractured leg and serious cuts and bruises. At the hospital, they were attended by their son, Dr. Harry Hund.[15]

Todd Nicol said that Carrie was never able to walk again without assistance and subsequently had to sleep in the downstairs bedroom at Freestone.

Frederick Hund died on 20 May 1941, followed by Carrie on 27 June 1941.

An obituary in the *San Anselmo Herald* said Dr. Hund "at one time was considered San Francisco's foremost surgeon."[16]

Their ashes were buried beneath a giant redwood tree on the Freestone property.

**Frederick and Carrie Hund, late 1930s
(Photo from Nicol Archives)**

Carrie, who was born on 26 August 1861 in San Francisco, was the daughter of Jacob Zech and Susan Grass, both German immigrants.

Jacob, a piano manufacturer, arrived in San Francisco in 1856, when the city was formally established. He was born in Durkheim, Bavaria on 25 July 1832 and naturalized as a U.S. citizen on 5 November 1860 in San Francisco.[17]

Susan Grass was born on 25 April 1831 in Hesse-Darmstadt.[18] She emigrated to New York in 1851.

An article in the archives of the San Francisco Museum says, "What a strange town was that, the San Francisco of 1856, its 30,000 people in speedy transition from a city of tents and shacks to one of brick and stone buildings."[19]

According to U.S. Census statistics, the California Gold Rush led to an explosion of the state's population. Between 1850 and 1860, it grew to 379,994.

The Gold Rush also led to the immigration of the James George Nicol family and the eventual union of Lawrence Nicol and Irene Hund—the daughter of Jacob Zech.

In an 1897 article, the *San Francisco Chronicle* said, "The first piano made in San Francisco was a six-octave square by Jacob Zech in 1856."[20]

The 1861 San Francisco city directory shows Zech at 529 California Street. He was joined in his business by his brother, Frederick Zech, in 1860.

An 1865 advertisement in the *San Francisco Chronicle* for Zech offered "a full assortment of Grand and Square Pianos constantly on hand. All orders for Tuning and Repairing promptly attended to."[21]

In the 1867 Pacific Coast Directory, he was listed at 419 Market St., occupation "Piano Forte Maker."[22]

He subsequently established his business at 211-213 Ninth St., where he worked until he retired in 1888. Zech died a year later. His wife, Susan, died in 1894.

**Jacob (left) and Frederick Zech, circa 1870
(Photo from Nicol Archives)**

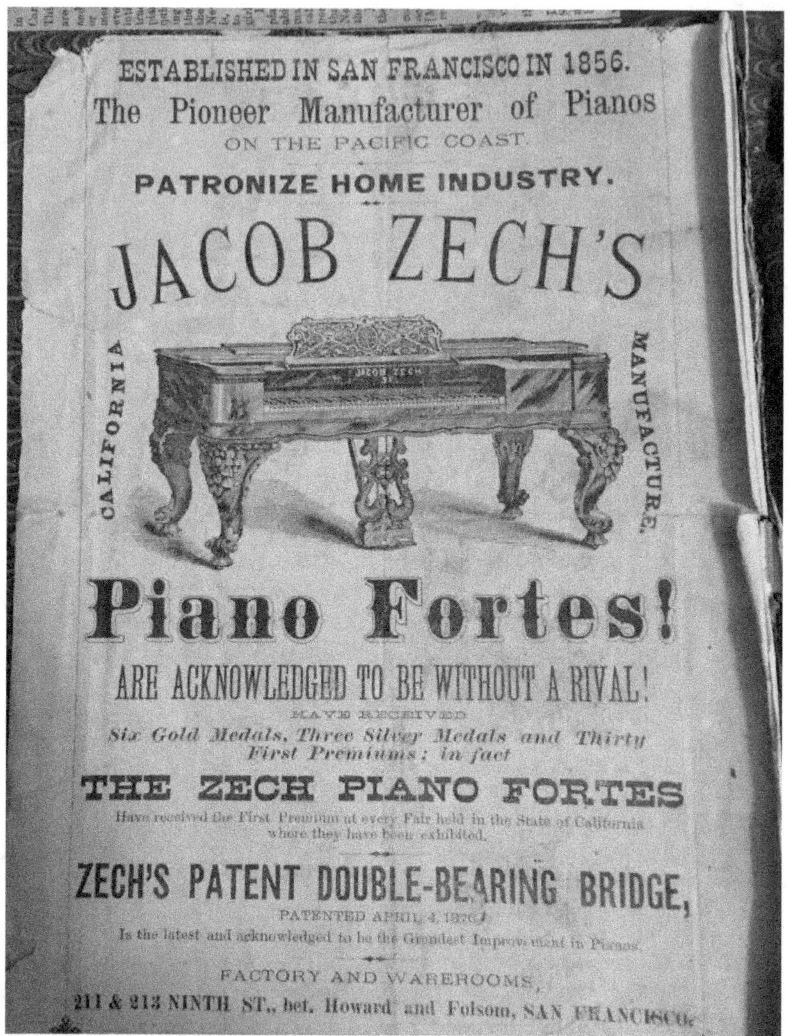

(Colville's San Francisco directory, 1857)
(Courtesy of the Museum of San Francisco)

6

Frank David Nicol

Frank David Nicol, the son of Lawrence and Irene Nicol, was born on 14 October 1921 in San Rafael, Marin County, California. The attending physician was Dr. Harry Hund, his uncle.[1]

Nicol was the grandson of Stockton attorney Frank David Nicol, whose father, James George Nicol, emigrated from Scotland to New Orleans in 1844.

By the time Frank was born, his parents were living on their almond ranch near Brentwood, in Contra Costa County. It was a far cry from the life he would have had in San Francisco, where his father had worked as an attorney.

"It was hard work," his daughter, Susan Nicol Thibodeaux said during an interview. "And it was boring. He couldn't wait to go to college. He had to wait a year, though, because I don't think they had the money to send him to Berkeley."[2]

Frank Nicol, 1938
(Photo from Nicol Archives)

Susan recalled Frank telling her he would have rather lived in San Francisco. The Nicol farm was remote at that time, but it was not far from Mount Diablo, which became important as aviation evolved.

"One story he told me, I believe it was in 1929, when aviation had just started," Susan said. "So they were putting a beacon on top of Mount Diablo, because, otherwise, aircraft were going to fly into the mountain. So there was this big buildup to when the beacon was first going to be lit. Dad told the story of how the three kids were out there waiting and waiting for it to go on."

Frank Nicol, Boy Scout, 1935
(Photo from Nicol Archives)

When he arrived at the University of California at Berkeley (Cal), Nicol was active in the Alpha Delta Phi fraternity and was an oarsman on the 1941 junior varsity rowing team that won the national championship in Poughkeepsie, New York.

It was by chance that Nicol made it to Poughkeepsie.

"He desperately wanted to go to the national finals at Poughkeepsie, but he wasn't in the first boat," Susan said. " He somehow convinced his parents that it was okay for him to stowaway in the baggage car to cross country. They really didn't want him to go. They wanted him to come home and work on the ranch for the summer. Somehow that got negotiated. He just said, 'I'm going.'"

Nicol made plans with another teammate to stow aboard the train in the baggage car, but shortly before the team departed, a member of the first boat team caught the measles.

"Frank was promoted to the first boat and the other guy had to stowaway in the baggage car," Susan said. "So they went across country, and they won the nationals."[3]

**Frank Nicol, Cal rowing team, 1941
(University of California Berkeley yearbook)**

During a 1974 interview with his daughter, Susan, Nicol said he enjoyed his time at Berkeley. "I was very happy there.

The boat crew, the letterman society, fraternity house, various campus service organizations."

Very few students had automobiles at Berkeley, he said. "Generally, everybody did everything. If you were going to have a football rally, everybody would go. Ten thousand people would go to the football rallies. The freshmen always wore a beanie."[4]

Nicol told Susan that he signed up for the Navy reserve program at Berkeley in 1942, shortly after the United States entered the war.

"I was in a Navy reserve program which allowed you to finish school, or until as such time as they needed you," he said.

On 6 June 1943, Nicol graduated with a B.A. in business administration and was commissioned as an officer in the U.S. Navy.

"I was in one Navy school after another for about a year," he said. "By the time I got through officer's school, it was late 1944."

After the war ended, he served as a torpedo officer on the U.S.S. McKean, which cleared Allied floating mines from Japanese waters. He said he was on the ship for about 18 months before his discharge.

**Lt. Frank Nicol, 1944
(Photo from Nicol Archives)**

After his discharge, Nicol worked in commercial sales for the Industrial Indemnity Insurance Company in San Francisco. While living in the city, he was a member of "The Bachelor's Club of San Francisco." On a dinner menu of the Palace Hotel on 14 April 1951, he was listed as one of five directors of the club.

An invitation for that dinner was sent by the club to Mr. and Mrs. Lawrence Nicol. The invitation card read: "It is requested that all men wear white dinner jackets."

In a 1953 article on the club in the *San Francisco Call-Bulletin*, titled "Among Those Who danced 'Til Dawn," the reporter wrote: "What can one say more than this: It was, as always, superb. A magnificent party. Here are some among this region's fairest and freshest, handsomest and most debonair who danced until dawn at the Bachelor's Ball.

"There were glad hellos for Frank Nicol, back from Los Angeles for the weekend, helping to check names at the narrow entrance."[5]

Nicol had moved to Los Angeles in 1953. While attending a Cal alumni association event, he met Jean Elliott, a 1945 Cal graduate who had been editor of *The Daily Californian* and president of the student body.

Although both had attended Cal in the early forties, they had never met. On 7 February 1954, they were married in the Garden Grove home of Jean's parents.[6]

Wedding Day, Garden Grove, CA., 1954
Left: Lawrence, Irene Nicol; Walter, Frank Nicol
Right: Raymond, Mary Lou, Jean Elliott
(Photo from Nicol Archives)

After living briefly in Pasadena, the Nicols moved to San Diego in 1955, where Nicol became a representative for St. Paul's Insurance. In 1962, Frank and a partner started a commercial insurance business, Hornaday-Nicol. He later worked in commercial sales for Barney & Barney insurance company in San Diego.

The Nicols had three children while living in San Diego: Susan, Todd and Alan.

In a 2022 interview in Tucson, Susan said the family lived on Point Loma, a seaside community within San Diego, in a home with "a little backyard with a swing set. Sometimes, in warm weather, we would play in the sprinklers."[7]

When they lived on Point Loma, vacations consisted of trips to northern California to visit the grandparents. It was a rare occasion when the family went out to a restaurant.

In a 30 December 1961 letter to family members, Frank extolled the virtues of living in the San Diego area:

"After seven years in three houses and three children all born here, we are confirmed San Diegans who believe all the Convention and Tourist Bureau superlatives and look with tolerance and sympathy on those forced to live elsewhere," he wrote.

At the same time, he noted in the letter, Jean at times felt overwhelmed by raising three children:

"Jean feels she spends most of her time acting as referee for small-fry battles, chauffeur to and from various lessons," he wrote, "and Florence Nightingale for all the skinned knees in the neighborhood."

The Nicol children, he wrote, "are alternately angels and hellions." [8]

**Jean and Frank Nicol, Pasadena, summer, 1954
(Photo from Nicol Archives)**

Jean, Frank, Alan, Susan, Todd Nicol, 1968
(Photo from Nicol Archives)

Nicol and his family moved to Sacramento in 1967, where he served as Director of the California Parks and Recreation Department, until 1969.

From 1969 through 1974, Nicol was Director of California Veterans Affairs, under Governor Ronald Reagan. The family then returned to San Diego, where Frank resumed his insurance career, after starting a small business with Jean, shipping gift boxes of avocados.

While living in San Diego, he was active in the Republican Party and was a delegate to the 1976 Republican National Convention.

Todd, Jean, Alan, Susan, Frank Nicol, 1979
(Photo from Nicol Archives)

In 1981, Frank and Jean Nicol bought property in Pauma Valley, located about 50 miles north of San Diego. They moved there a few years later, after their house was built.

Frank was a very social man, with numerous friends in Pauma Valley. At Happy Hour, he always made sure his guests had a drink and showed a genuine interest in people.

Even in his 90s, Frank still tried to keep up his physical fitness. A few years before he died, Frank told me his goal was to do fifty push-ups a day. I'm not certain that he achieved his goal, but I have no doubt he tried.

Frank was very independent and reluctant to leave his home in Pauma Valley, despite his increasing frailty.

On 28 April 2015, Frank passed away, after moving from his Pauma Valley home to an assisted living residence in nearby Escondido. His last few weeks were spent in a hospice in the same home where his wife, Jean lived.

He died in the same bedroom occupied by Jean, before she passed away.

Frank was 93.

Susan Nicol Thibodeaux and Frank Nicol, 2012
(Photo by John T. Young)

**Frank Nicol at Berkeley, 1943
(Photo from Nicol Archives)**

**Jean and Frank Nicol, 1995
(Photo from Nicol Archives)**

7

Board's Crossing

In the early 1900s, Stockton attorney Frank David Nicol traveled east in his horse-drawn buggy from Stockton to a river crossing in the Sierra Nevadas known as Board's Crossing, located on the north fork of the Stanislaus River.

Nicol may have learned about Board's Crossing from his father, James George Nicol, who would stop at the river to fish while returning from Carson City, Nevada via Ebbetts Pass, according to Todd Nicol. Todd said James took up farming near Columbia after the gold mines played out and sold wagon loads of fruit to Nevada miners.

Todd said his great-grandfather, Frank, bought Board's Crossing and 160 acres of land surrounding it for $2,000. Nicol had a partner, Dr. W.G. Wallace of Stockton, who later sold his share back to Nicol. The property became a family legacy that has continued through many generations of Nicols.[1]

A 1907 article in *The Evening Mail* about the Board's Crossing sale said Nicol "is an enthusiastic lover of the woods and streams, and has often expressed the opinion that the region around the Big Trees and Gardner's was the ideal fishing portion of the State."

The article went on to say that Nicol and Wallace "are going to build a wagon road from Gardner's down to their resort—not a mere trail but a good substantial roadway for carriages and heavier vehicles."

Nicol and Wallace, the article said, planned "to establish a little tent town there, and will have accommodations sufficient to entertain some of their friends."[2]

The "Gardner's" referenced in the article pertains to John Gardner and William Gibson, who bought a 160-acre property on Highway 4 in 1868.

Gardner built a hotel and opened a general store. It was known as Gardner's Station when a post office was established in 1902, but the name was changed to Dorrington. It was the last stopping off place for those enroute to Board's Crossing.[3]

Board's Crossing was established on the Stanislaus River in the early 1870s by David and William Board, who arrived there from Missouri in 1854. The shallow ford across the river was used by local ranchers who moved their cattle into the mountains during the summer.

An historic marker near the bridge at Board's crossing says the property was sold to Nicol in 1906. The marker has one error: Nicol was misspelled "Nichols."

**Board's Crossing Historic Site
(Photo by John T. Young)**

A bridge was built across the river in 1926, and ranchers began running their cattle across the bridge, which connects Calaveras and Tuolumne counties. The aging bridge is scheduled for maintenance by the U.S. Forest Service. Three engineers from the Forest Service examined it in 2021, but they told Susan Nicol Thibodeaux they could not say when the bridge will be refurbished because funds for the project were not yet available.

Board's Crossing Bridge, 2022
(Photo by John T. Young)

"I can remember as a kid, herds of cattle coming through here," said Todd Nicol, during an interview at Board's Crossing in 2021. He often visited the Nicol property with his family in the 1970s. "That's why the road barrier is pushed up, by the bridge. Too many cattle balking."

When fishing at Board's Crossing, Frank D. Nicol stayed at a nearby cabin built by the Board family. Only a few years after buying the property, however, Nicol's health began to fail. He died on 10 March 1910 in Stockton.[4] An article in the *San Francisco Call* said he had been in poor health for several years and seriously ill for several months.[5] He was 51.

With Nicol's passing, the property was bequeathed to his wife, Adelaide Dodge Nicol. Adelaide later sold the Board's Crossing land to her son-in-law, Robert Hays Smith, who married Adelaide's daughter, Susan Alice Nicol, in 1908. In

1936, during the Great Depression, Smith went bankrupt and lost the land to Wells Fargo Bank.

Nicol Smith, their son, married Moira Archibold on 2 June 1938 in Washington, D.C.[6] An heiress to the Standard Oil fortune, Moira helped Nicol acquire the property back from the bank in 1939, according to Sharon Karr, author of *Traveler of the Crossroads*, a biography of Nicol Smith.[7]

After Nicol Smith died in 1995, he bequeathed the property to his first cousin, Frank Nicol. When Frank passed away in 2015, the property was jointly inherited by Frank's children, Susan, Todd, and Alan.

Nicol residence, Board's Crossing, 2021
(Photo by John T. Young)

A 1938 article in *The San Francisco Examiner* about the upcoming nuptials of Nicol and Moira said that after the wedding, "the newlyweds will sail on the Europa for a summer in Europe. They will first visit Norway and Sweden, then go to Russa." Before returning to America, the article said they would spend time in France, "where both have many friends."[8]

In 1939, Nicol Smith built the first of two homes at Board's Crossing. The original house was a three-bedroom, two-story residence built with a foundation of river rock, taken from the banks of the Stanislaus River. The interior was lined with golden knotty pine.

A small bedroom was located in the attic, and a maid's room, complete with bathroom, was built in the basement. The main floor upstairs included two bathrooms, a living room with fireplace, a pantry room and a kitchen. A propane tank provides fuel for the stove, lights, refrigerator and heaters.

Nicol living room, Board's Crossing, 2020
(Photo by John T. Young)

In the living room, a charcoal portrait of Nicol Smith and his dog rests on one wall, next to a photo of Nicol and his parents, taken when he was about one year old.

Sliding glass double doors lead to a wooden deck that overlooks the river, and enormous ponderosa and sugar pine trees loom over the property.

A cement walkway leads to a paved landing, where Nicol Smith hosted numerous parties. He built a second, contiguous home in 1959, now known as the "Owner's House," but known as "Nicol's House" when he lived. The upper floor is composed of a large bedroom with a bathroom, while the downstairs was designed for social gatherings.

The house did not have a kitchen because Nicol's cook prepared the meals in the original house next door.

A writing desk for Nicol Smith rested near a large bay window overlooking the Stanislaus River, just 25 yards away. Smith was a travel lecturer and author of several books, including a best-seller, "Burma Road."

Smith was born on 10 January 1910 in the Fairmont Hotel in San Francisco to Susan and Robert Hays Smith. He graduated from Stanford University in 1933 and embarked on a lifelong career as an adventurer and travel writer. He was one of the first Americans to take motion pictures of Angel Falls in Venezuela.

Until the outbreak of World War II, Smith made his living as a lecturer, discussing his travel adventures at many American universities and around the world.

On his WWII draft card, Nicol listed his address as "Apartment, Hotel St. Francis, San Francisco." He listed his employer as William Colston Leigh Sr. who created one of the world's leading speaker's agencies, the W. Colston Leigh Bureau.[9]

During World War II, Smith served in Gen. William Donovan's Office of Strategic Services (OSS), the precursor to the CIA. In Thailand, he helped organize an underground resistance to fight the Japanese.

Lt. Col Nicol Smith, OSS, 1945
(Photo from Nicol Archives)

In an August 1943 letter from Nicol to his parents, published in *The San Francisco Examiner*, he said, "My house is at the edge of a river. I am deep in primitive jungle. The rains have started and they never stop. My house is unbelievably primitive. The walls are of mud, and the roof of thatch."[10]

After a hike through the jungle, he wrote, "I discovered that some twenty-five leeches had worked their way under the leggings and my right leg was a mass of blood."

In another letter to his parents, which was published in *The San Francisco Examiner* on 5 September 1943, Smith said he had suffered from malaria for three weeks. "The food is meager and very hard to get," he said. "My waist is now thirty-two instead of thirty-six. I weigh about 158 pounds instead of the 190 when I was married."[11]

By November 1943, Smith had been promoted to major and was in Chungking, China preparing newly-arrived OSS agents for undercover work in Thailand. The training schedule included cryptography, physical training, weapons, and parachute training.

A declassified letter dated 17 November 1943 from a senior OSS agent said, "Japs know some of the plans about sending equipment and men into country by air, sea, plane and sub."[12] The letter highlighted the risk the OSS agents faced in Thailand. The government of Thailand supported Japan at the outset of the war, so the OSS agents faced not only the Japanese soldiers but also the Thai military and police.

Prior to the arrival of the OSS agents, American military commanders had little knowledge of Japanese troop strength and movements in Thailand. Nicol Smith and other OSS agents had to form relationships with a group of Thais who had been studying in America. Those Thais were covertly dispatched to Thailand with Smith and his colleagues to create networks of agents in the country.

Aside from his bouts with malaria, Nicol survived the war unscathed. He left for China in March 1943 and did not return to America until August 1945, when OSS commander William Donovan awarded him the Legion of Merit for his wartime service in Thailand.

After the war, Nicol hosted many parties at Board's Crossing, and one of his frequent guests was his first cousin, Frank Nicol, who lived in San Francisco. Susan Nicol Thibodeaux said her father became good friends with Nicol. Both were very social and veterans of World War II.

Born into the high society of San Francisco, Nicol had numerous friends who were celebrities. Actors Gary Cooper, and Ray Bolger stayed at Nicol's Board Crossing home for the weekend, along with Herb Caen, a columnist for *The San Francisco Chronicle.*

Another famous guest was Elsa Maxwell, who was a gossip columnist, author, and songwriter from New York. She was credited for the introduction of the scavenger hunt at party games.

Nicol's mother, Susan Nicol Smith, was a society columnist for *The San Francisco Examiner.* In her 1959 obituary, the *Examiner* wrote that she was "the confidant of the socially elite in California, New York, London, Paris and elsewhere."[13]

The obituary included excerpts of a letter Susan wrote to a friend in 1936, when she began writing her column:

"I do hope I can put across the picture of society as it is today, with stuffed-shirt formality gone forever, with amusement the keynote and brains and charm the passports.

"I want in my column to pay tribute, too, to those hostesses we know so well, for the graciousness and charm, the distinction and flavor they have given to life in San Francisco."

Susan Nicol Smith, circa 1908
(Photo from Nicol Archives)

Access to Board's Crossing was along a three-mile dirt road that was carved from the original cattle trail. The village of Dorrington, several miles beyond the dirt road turnoff, had the only telephone in the area. No telephone or electric lines existed then or now at Board's Crossing.

Before the war, numerous residents from surrounding communities camped just down the river from Nicol's property. Some of them helped construct his first home.

One local, Art Hall, built Nicol's house in 1939. Nicol met Hall by chance at a bank in Patterson, California in 1933. Hall, a rancher in the Patterson area, had graduated from Santa

Monica High School and had some friends from there in common with Nicol.

After the war, Hall ran Nicol's film projection equipment and acted as his chauffeur between lecture locations, until Bill Green took on that role. Hall later became Nicol's photographer and filmmaker, accompanying him around the world on his trips for the next several decades.

When he returned from the war, Nicol provided leases to the campers and forged friendships with them. For his parties, Nicol hired young people from the camps to help prepare food and drinks and rake the sand and pine needles around his home.

Nicol's frequent absences took a toll on his marriage to Moira, who filed for divorce in 1952. As part of the divorce settlement, Nicol was awarded the Board's Crossing property and an annual payment of $4,000 per year. Moira's family were heirs to the Standard Oil fortune and helped finance many of Nicol's trips overseas.

In 1962, the Stanislaus National Forest and Sierra Pacific Industries built the Sourgrass Bridge over the Stanislaus River, several miles north of Board's Crossing. Later, a new paved road led over the bridge and toward a logging area a few miles away. From a crest on the road, a new dirt road wound down the hill about a mile to Board's Crossing.

The Sourgrass Bridge was destroyed by a flood in 1997 but was rebuilt two years later. A photo in the Nicol residence shows water reaching the edge of the house during the flood.

Board's Crossing, Stanislaus River, 2022
(Photo by John T. Young)

During the late 1960s, Frank Nicol brought his family to Board's Crossing for summer vacations. Susan, his daughter, recalled that Nicol had "a big, round face, round belly, and was chatty, always."

Her brother, Alan, recalled the time when Nicol lost his hearing aid:

"One summer when I was at the river Nicol Smith stuck his head out the upstairs window of his house and shouted, 'One-hundred dollars to anyone who can find my hearing aid. I can't see well without my hearing aid.' I found it on his nightstand. I passed on the $100."[14]

After Frank Nicol inherited the Board's Crossing property in 1995 he and his family began spending more time there during the summers.

In a 12 July 2005 letter to his family, Frank wrote, "The weather was perfect. . .all of our younger guests went down the rapids on the rubber tires. . .mountains of food & drink goodies all weekend. . .All hands raked pine needles. See what you missed?"[15]

A 20 September 2005 letter from Frank to his family highlighted the potential hazards in the woods around Board's Crossing.

"Near the camps on the Tuolumne County side, a mountain lion killed a deer, then buried it for later feast," he wrote. "A camper saw the deer's feet sticking out of the cover, went to investigate and was greeted by a snarling, most unfriendly mountain lion on guard."[16]

The following year, Frank noted in a 20 July 2006 letter, his granddaughter, Avery Nicol, was swinging on a rope tied underneath the bridge when the rope broke.

"And down she went into the water," Frank wrote. Avery hit the rocks, "which gave her two very painful, but fixable knees."[17]

A few months later, Frank asked his son, Alan, to get rid of a skunk in the basement of the guest house at Board's Crossing.

"He found it—very dead when he pushed a shovel on top the animal, and a mouse jumped out, hissed at Alan, who reared back and hit his head on the overhead," Frank wrote. "Alan consigned the skunk to the River, then sealed the entry hole."[18]

In a 2007 letter, Frank alluded to the constant upkeep required to maintain the homes at Board's Crossing.

"Keeping up with the work on the River is much for Jean and Frank. The boys perform much repair work there, but always more to do," he wrote.[19]

Since the passing of their parents, Susan, Todd and Alan Nicol have stayed at Board's Crossing throughout the summers. They rake leaves and pine needles, make repairs on the homes, and following a long-established Nicol tradition, invite guests down to The River, as they call their home.

Over the last few decades of his life, Nicol Smith sold most of his property. When he passed away on 18 May 1995, he left the remaining three acres of riverfront property to his cousin, Frank Nicol, along with water rights to acreage nearby. He left the campground properties to Art Hall.

In 1994, Sharon Karr published *Traveler Crossroads*, her biography about Nicol Smith. In a 1995 column in the *San Francisco Chronicle*, Herb Caen wrote that Art Hall had received an advance copy of the book.

Caen said Hall "settled down in bed to read it. At 2 a.m. he fell asleep. His wife, Virginia, tried in vain to awaken him. At age 85, Art Hall, Nicol Smith's buddy, had died with his friend's story still in his hands."[20]

Virginia, Art's wife, inherited the campgrounds and passed them along to Art's daughter, Patty Koehn, and his grandson, Eric Koehn.

The campsites are frequently used during warm weather by several generations of descendants who travel to Board's Crossing from throughout California. Many of the adults who now lease campsites from Eric Koehn played on the river as children.

**Susan Nicol Thibodeaux, Board's Crossing, 2020
(Photo by John T. Young)**

**Frankie Nicol, Sue's dog, Board's Crossing, 2022
(Photo by Susan Nicol Thibodeaux)**

8

Dodge and Rogers

On 30 July 1883, Frank David Nicol married Adelaide Louise Dodge in Tuolumne County.[1] Adelaide was born in Tuolumne County in 1861, the daughter of Dr. Mark Tyler Dodge and Eliza Rogers. Dr. Dodge died at age 34 in 1866, when Adelaide was only five years old.

By age 19, she was living in San Francisco with her mother. According to the 1880 U.S. Census, Adelaide and her mother, Eliza, were living at 320 22nd Street with Nelson Rogers, Adelaide's uncle.[2]

Since Frank and Adelaide were only two years apart in age, it's likely they met in Tuolumne County before she moved to San Francisco. He grew up in Columbia, and she lived in Jamestown, both close to the county seat of Sonora.

In 1880, Frank began his law practice in Sonora, so it's likely he maintained a relationship with Adelaide after she moved to San Francisco.

Adelaide's father, Dr. Mark Dodge, was born in New York on 14 May 1832. In 1855, he married Eliza Rogers in Jamestown, Tuolumne County.[3]

Dodge came from a family of physicians. His father, Jonathan, was born in Connecticut and lived in New York, where he was a physician. After his father died in 1854, Mark, moved to Jamestown.

His brother, also a physician, had already moved to Jamestown. Dr. Jonathan Dodge arrived in San Francisco on the steamship *Columbus* on 17 June 1852.[4] He apparently returned to New York in 1855 and married Caroline Ballentine. According to his burial records, Jonathan and Caroline had two children, Jonathan and Sophia Dodge, both born in New York.

Jonathan died in 1859 in Jamestown, at age 30; records indicate that his body was returned to New York for burial.[5]

No records were available to explain why Mark and his brother Jonathan died so young. Dr. Jonathan Dodge of New York, the father of the two Jamestown physicians, died at age 54, and Jonathan's father, Daniel Dodge, died at age 50. Jonathan's sisters fared better. Frances Dodge died in 1904, at age 77 and Caroline Adelaide Dodge lived at least until 1910, age 79.

In a letter written to Mark Dodge in 1862, Caroline expressed her concern about the Civil War, which began in 1861. She had moved from New York to Illinois with her husband, Archibald Tredway.

"Everything here today is in an awful state of confusion and excitement as regards 'War.' There is nothing else thought of or talked of: war meetings, bounties, volunteering and drafting are the order of the day," she wrote.

"I love my country and regret exceedingly the wretched state were are in, but I have so little else to love—my husband, God forever bless him, and my darling only brother," Caroline continued. "I can't give either up."

"Do they talk of drafting in California?" she asked. "Do tell me all, that you feel or think or know in relation to this terrible subject."

In Caroline's letter, it was clearly evident that she was close to her brother: "If I could see you face to face for one little hour I think my heart would not be so hungry. How is wife and little ones—is my precious namesake well?"[6]

The namesake she referred to was Adelaide Dodge, who was born in Tuolumne County in February 1861.

No records indicate that Dr. Mark Dodge served in the army during the Civil War. According to *History.com*, some 17,000 Californians served as Union soldiers, while only a few hundred joined the Confederacy.

Mark's brother, Jonathan, died before the war began. Jonathan's medical practice was in Jamestown, where he charged $20 a visit, according to *In Pursuit of the Golden Dream*, by Howard Gardiner.

In his book, Gardiner relates the story of Tim Matchin, who was suffering from inflammation of the prostate. His pain "was incessant day and night, and the only way I could find relief was in the use of powerful narcotics."

Matchin went to see Dr. Jonathan Dodge, who promised to perform surgery to fix his problem. "He was a jolly fellow," Matchin wrote, "whose confidence in his ability to cure me so encouraged me, that I felt safe in following his advice."

When he woke up from the surgery, Matchin said, "What a luxury it was to feel for the first time in weeks free from pain."

He said Dr. Dodge handed him a cigar and told him to make himself comfortable.

Although Dodge advised his patient to avoid alcohol, he came to his room at his hotel with a bottle, poured him a drink and said, "This is good, it will do you no harm, but beware of the rotgut downstairs."[7]

His patient, Tim Matchin, was elected Lt. Governor of California from 1863 to 1867. He represented Tuolumne and Mono counties in the California State Assembly in 1862 and 1863.

Before leaving New York on 18 June 1854, Dr. Jonathan Dodge applied for membership in the Sons of the American Revolution, based on the service of his grandfather, Daniel Dodge, who was born on 19 July 1757 in New London, Connecticut.

Daniel Dodge, according to U.S. Revolutionary War rolls, was a corporal in the 1st Regiment of the Connecticut militia. He joined on 3 January 1778, at age 20.[8] He was a descendant of Tristam Dodge, who arrived in Rhode Island in 1661 from Suffolk, England.[9]

Adelaide Dodge's brother, Washington H. Dodge, was also a physician. Born on 3 June 1859 in Jamestown, Dodge lived with his uncle Edwin Rogers, a lawyer in Sonora, after his father died in 1866. Based on U.S. census records, it appears that Edwin and his brother Nelson, in San Francisco, assumed some responsibility for Eliza Rogers and her children.

Dodge attended the Boys High School in San Francisco, while living with his uncle, Nelson Rogers, a businessman who was born in Vermont in 1834. According to the 1870 U.S. Census, Rogers was living in San Francisco and was an "expressman," someone who ensured the safe delivery of gold or currency.[10]

In the 1880 U.S. Census, Dodge, age 21, listed his address as Sonora and his occupation as teacher.[11] He soon moved back to San Francisco, where he graduated from the medical department of the University of California in 1884. He later became a member of the medical department's faculty with the title of Professor of Therapeutics.[12]

Dodge entered political life in 1898, when he was elected supervisor in San Francisco County. Two years later, he was elected county assessor, a position he held for four successive terms. He retired from politics to become vice president of the Anglo-London and Paris National Bank in April 1912[13]

Following a trip to France, Dodge, his wife Ruth, and their four-year-old son, Washington Dodge Jr, boarded the *Titanic* on 14 April 1912 for its maiden voyage from Southampton, England to New York. Many of the ship's builders claimed that the ship was unsinkable. Onboard were some 2,200 people, of whom 1,300 were passengers.

Just before midnight, the ship struck an iceberg, and at least five of its supposedly watertight compartments were ruptured. As attempts were made to contact nearby ships, the crew began to launch lifeboats.

"My wife awakened me and said that something had happened to the ship," Dodge said on April 19 during a talk the Hotel Wolcott in New York. "We went on deck and everything seemed quiet and orderly. The orchestra was playing a lively tune. They started to lower the lifeboats after a lapse of some minutes."[14]

Hundreds of passengers and crew fell into the icy water. More than 1,500 people perished; the Dodge family survived.

Der Untergand de Titanic, 1912
(Courtesy of German magazine Die Gartenlaube)

After six or seven lifeboats were lowered, Dodge said, passengers began to panic. "Some of the passengers fought with such desperation to get into the lifeboats that the officers shot them, and their bodies fell into the ocean," Dodge said during his speech at the Hotel Wolcott in New York.[15]

After he returned home, Dr. Dodge was interviewed by *The Californian.* He said "the great loss of life was due as much to the lack of men to operate the boats as it was of lack of boats to take off the people." After putting his wife and son in a boat, he said he was "one of the last to leave the doomed liner."[16]

As numerous investigations of the disaster unfolded, Dodge was criticized for taking a lifeboat when some women still remained aboard. In a speech about the *Titanic* to the

Commonwealth Club of San Francisco on 12 May 1912, Dodge defended his actions. He said he watched lifeboats being lowered on the starboard side of the ship.

"I watched all boats on the starboard side, comprising the odd numbers from 1 to 13 as they were launched," he said. "Not a boat was launched which could not have held from ten to twenty-five more persons." During this time, Dodge helped his wife, Ruth, and their son, Washington Dodge, Jr., 4, into lifeboat 5. He stayed behind.

After assisting about eight women into lifeboat 13 on the starboard side, he said the officer in charge repeatedly called for more women but none appeared. "The men were told to tumble in. Along with those present I entered the boat."[17]

Dodge's account was backed up by a U.S. Senate inquiry, during which senators took testimony from survivors. Dining Room Steward Frederick Ray, who had served the Dodge family during the voyage, said he pushed Dr. Dodge into the lifeboat.

"He was standing well back from the boat, and I said, you had better get in here, then. I got behind him and pushed him, and I followed,." Ray told the senators.[18]

Ray said lifeboat 13 contained about two-thirds women and one-third men. The women, he said, were from the second and third class sections of the *Titanic*.

The lowering of the boat, Ray said, was hazardous because of a "solid mass of water pouring from a hole in the side of the ship." The men grabbed oars and pushed away from the ship.

"It seemed impossible to lower the boat without being swamped; we pushed it out from the side of the ship and the next I knew we were in the water," Ray said.

Dodge said there were no officers or sailors on his boat and progress was "extremely slow." As his boat moved away from the Titanic, Dodge said he could hear the screams of passengers who were "perishing in those icy waters."[19]

Ray also verified Dodge's account that no officers or sailors were on the boat. "Nobody seemed to take command of the boat, so we elected a fireman to take charge," Ray said. "He ordered us to put out the oars and pull straightaway from the ship."

A transcript of his speech to the Commonwealth Club noted that when Dodge spoke about those passengers who were screaming, he "broke down, and with difficulty proceeded with the narrative."[20]

At 4:45 a.m. that morning his boat was rescued by the ship *Carpathia.* His wife and son arrived at the ship at 5:10 a.m. His son was hauled up in a mail sack onto the deck.

"A steward rushed up with coffee, but Master Dodge announced he would rather have cocoa," said Walter Lord in his book, *A Night to Remember.* "The steward promptly dashed off and got some—British liners aren't famous for their service for nothing."[21]

In August 1912, Dodge resigned as County Assessor. In a letter printed in *The Recorder*, San Francisco Mayor James Rolph, Jr. said, "The resignation of Dr. Washington Dodge withdraws from the public service one of the ablest and most efficient officials San Francisco has ever known."

Rolph added, "During his incumbency, he has vastly elevated the officer of Assessor in importance, dignity and effectiveness. He has enjoyed the full confidence of the public."[22]

Dodge continued working as vice president of the Anglo-London and Paris National Bank.

In 1918, he purchased some property contiguous to the West Point Inn, located near the top of Mt. Tamalpais in Marin County. The property sits atop the 2,500-foot mountain, with a 360-degree view from the San Francisco Bay to the Pacific Ocean.

The Inn was built in 1904, where the Mt. Tamalpais Scenic Railway met a horse-drawn stagecoach.[23]

Dodge built what is known as the "Honeymoon Cabin," a one-bedroom cabin with its own bathroom. According to the West Point Inn history site, Dodge's cabin was the last built on the property.

Dodge later donated his property to the Marin Municipal Water District, and the West Point Inn is now listed on the National Register of Historic Places. The Inn is now a destination for hikers.

In 1919, Dodge was sued by two men who claimed that he persuaded them to purchase thousands of shares in the Poulsen Wireless Company at inflated prices.

On 22 June 1919, *The San Francisco Examiner* reported that Dodge shot himself in the garage of his home at 840 Powell St. in San Francisco. He died at St. Francis Hospital on 30 June 1919, according to funeral records. He was 60.

While some observers believed he committed suicide over guilt at surviving the *Titanic* disaster, his attorney, Gavin McNab, said Dodge was distraught over the lawsuit filed against him over the sale of stock of the Poulsen Wireless Company.

"Dr. Dodge cared nothing about the financial side of the suit," McNab said, "but the assault upon his good name overcame him,"[24] he told the *Examiner.*

Dr. Washington Dodge, circa 1900
(Photo from Nicol Archives)

Dodge did not leave a suicide note or tell anyone why he planned to shoot himself, so his reasons may never be known.

In 1910, two years before the *Titanic* disaster, Frank D. Nicol died in Stockton. His wife, Adelaide, and her mother, Eliza Rogers Dodge—the mother of Dr. Washington Dodge—subsequently moved to San Francisco, where they shared an apartment.

After Frank and Adelaide moved to Stockton in 1888, Eliza had moved in with them. Adelaide was in poor health, and Eliza helped to care for their children.

Born on 13 September 1836 in Newbury, Vermont, Eliza left home at age 18 and traveled to San Francisco in March 1854 via the Isthmus of Panama. According to family accounts, she rode a mule across Panama to the Pacific Ocean, where she boarded the steamship *Uncle Sam*.

She was accompanied on her trip by a family friend, Judge Leander Quint, a pioneer of Tuolumne County. Eliza subsequently lived in Jamestown with her brother, Edwin Rogers, a lawyer.

Edwin, a graduate of Harvard, came to California in 1852 and briefly tried his luck mining gold. He was admitted as a member of the bar of Tuolumne County on 20 June 1854.

In a letter written to her mother on 28 May 1854, Eliza said, "We live on a beautiful hill some one hundred rods back from the main street, so that we hear none of the noise during the day, and the 'Fandangos' do not trouble us at nights.

"I always have the revolver loaded nearby, but have no fear of having occasion to use it. I have learned to shoot quite well as I have a mark to shoot at, fixed up at the back door.

"There has not been a man shot in this place for the last seven weeks. Before this they have averaged one in two weeks for the last five years."[25]

**Eliza Rogers Dodge, date unknown
(Photo from Nicol Archives)**

Eliza's grandson, Lawrence Nicol, said her experience with guns came in handy when she lived with his family in Stockton.

"A great many tramps used to come down from Sacramento," he said. "Our house was burglarized three times. One night she heard a noise about midnight in the kitchen. Instead of rousing father, she took a pistol and slipped down to the back stairway. She opened the door to the kitchen and this fellow flew out, and she took a shot at him.

"The next morning we found that he had carved a hole through the back door so he could get his hand in there," Nicol said. "She didn't say much about it. I guess women had to be that way at that time or they wouldn't survive. She was a pretty woman, but she had a mind more like a man."[26]

Why did Eliza leave home at age 18 and set out on a such a perilous journey? Her father, Josiah Rogers, died in 1846, when she only 9. Her mother, Lydia Aldrich Rogers, then married William Bolton, a widower who had two other children.[27]

While no records exist to indicate the nature of Eliza's relationship with her stepfather, it is likely that she was looking for an opportunity to strike out on her own. Her brother Edwin in Jamestown provided that opportunity.

According to an obituary in the *East Barre Record* in Vermont in 1898, Edwin Rogers became a judge in Sonora. Quoting from a eulogy given in Sonora, the article said:

"His face and manner were alike uncommon. There was much about him to remind you of the old Roman: the cast of head, the classic features, the fiery and restive nature, the moral and personal daring, the political temperament and uncompromising support of the cause he followed."[28]

Eliza's grandson, Lawrence Nicol, recalled meeting Rogers in Sonora, when he was a young boy. He said somebody tried to assassinate him, apparently over a dispute about a gold mine.

"He was walking up the street, in front of the old brick building where his office was," Nicol said. "He got about halfway up and someone, a would-be assassin sprang out and shot at him point blank. It struck his watch, which reflected the bullet and knocked him down. Saved his life."[29]

Another account of the incident, perhaps more accurate, was written in *The History of Tuolumne County, California*, by B.F. Alley, in 1882. Alley wrote that Rogers was the attorney for the Bonanza Mine, which was sued over its ownership of a gold mine. Alley said that Rogers "was the victim of a midnight assassin, who, on the evening of September 20, waylaid him near his residence and fired a shot."

The shot "entered the back to the right of the spinal column, and passing around the ribs, came out in front."

While the wound was initially thought to be fatal, it was not. After a few weeks, Rogers recovered. "The identity of the assailant has not so far been established," Alley wrote.[30]

Edwin Rogers died on 29 June 1898 in San Francisco, at age 64. An obituary in the *Los Angeles Times* described him as "a prominent attorney of Sonora, Tuolumne County, and one of the leading Masons of the State."[31]

The Grand Lodge of the Masons said Mark Tyler Dodge was expelled from St. James Lodge No 54 in 1866, the year he died. In a letter sent to Jean Nicol in 1978, the Grand Lodge of the Masons said most Masonic records for California were destroyed in the San Francisco earthquake of 1906; no further information was available on why Dodge was expelled from the lodge.[32]

It is likely that Dodge and his brother-in-law, Edwin Rogers belonged to the same lodge in Sonora, but no records exist to indicate whether Rogers was involved in the expulsion of Dodge. Or if he tried to defend him.

Eliza Rogers Dodge died in San Francisco on 01 May 1925. Her great-grandfather, Josiah Rogers, was born on 11 April 1749 in Rockingham, New Hampshire. He enlisted in the 3rd Regiment of the New Hampshire Militia on 16 January 1778,[33] just 13 days after Daniel Dodge joined the Connecticut militia.

Josiah Rogers was the descendant of Robert Rogers, who was born on 11 January 1617 in Somerset, England and died on 23 December 1663 in Newbury, Massachusetts.[34]

9

Jean Elliott

Jean Katherine Elliott was born 21 December 1923 in Los Angeles County, the daughter of Raymond Davis Elliott and Mary Lou Sherrill.[1] She would marry Frank Nicol in 1954.

By 1925, the Elliott family was living in Long Beach, at 2200 Eucalyptus Street. In 1927, Jean's brother, John was born.

Jean graduated from Long Beach Polytechnic High School in 1941. The school's website claims it is "nationally recognized as the home of scholars and champions."

In her 1941 senior yearbook, Jean was noted for activities with the "Chamber of Commerce."[2] The yearbook said, "The purpose of this organization is to promote friendliness and cooperation among the students."

Jean was also featured as a member of the "Girl's League Executive Board." The aim of the league was "to promote higher ideals among the girls of Poly High."

Jean Elliott, age 18
(Photo from Nicol Archives)

The Elliott home was about one and a half miles from Polytechnic High School.

In a letter about her brother, John, for his eulogy in 2001, Jean said that she and John "body-surfed in the summer" while growing up in Long Beach, which she described as "a small town then, and an important oil production center."

The Elliott home was located about three miles from the beach, which runs several miles along Ocean Blvd. to Belmont Shore. Jean and John likely used buses to reach the beach; trolley cars ran until the mid-1930s, when the tracks were removed, according to the Long Beach Public Library.

**Long Beach, Belmont Shore, 1930s
(Photo courtesy of Long Beach Public Library)**

She noted that her father, Raymond was in the oil well servicing business, and that he once taught chemistry and coached football at Polytechnic High School. Raymond moved to California from Ohio in 1912 and taught at the school until 1916.

When Jean graduated, war had already begun in Europe and East Asia. Hitler invaded Poland in 1939, and Japan attacked China in 1937. Few people predicted the Japanese attack on Pearl Harbor on 7 December 1941, but many Americans believed the United States would soon be at war. A foreword in the 1941 yearbook said:

"In view of the strained international relations prevailing in the world during this past year it seems only fitting that we, as true Americans, should strive to further a more universal appreciation of the great country in which we live."[3]

After graduating from high school., Jean attended the University of California at Berkeley (Cal). By the end of her first semester, America was at war with Japan and Germany.

In 1944, she was president of the student body and editor of *The Daily Californian*. She was also a member of Theta Sigma Phi sorority.

As a senior, Jean was a member of the Mortar Board, a national honor society recognizing college seniors for their "exemplary scholarship, leadership and service."

In a 1974 interview with her daughter, Susan, Jean said World War II resulted in major changes in life at Berkeley.

"From a school of eighteen or twenty thousand, it got down to six or seven thousand," she said. "There was the ROTC program. So there were quite a few men on campus, but they were in uniform.

"You went to school year around," she said. "You had a week off between semesters. If you went out to dinner, you had to be in by seven o'clock, and lights out by ten."

Jean graduated with a B.A. in Journalism from Cal. In 1947, she worked for the Voice of America in New York. She listed her occupation as "newspaperwoman," and lived at 117 W. 58th St.

The VOA, which is funded by the U.S. government, began broadcasting news in 1942 to combat Nazi propaganda. After World War II, VOA developed broadcasts aimed at countering communism and the Soviet Union.

Jean Elliott, age 22
(Photo from Nicol Archives)

In 1953, when she met Frank Nicol, Jean was working at the Cal alumni office in Pasadena. Frank and Jean were married on 7 Feb 1954 in the Garden Grove home of Jean's parents.

According to an article in *The San Francisco Examiner*, "The bridal gown was a Cahill original styled with a lace bodice appliqued with Chantilly lace and a blush pink tulle skirt of ballerina length. Her shoulder-length veil fell from a Juliet cap of pearls on satin and lace."[4]

The newlyweds had a reception at the Newport Harbor Yacht Club in Balboa. After a brief stay in Pasadena, the couple moved to San Diego, where Frank worked for Traveler's Insurance Company.

For the next several decades, Jean was busy raising three children: Susan was born in 1955, followed by Todd in 1957 and Alan in 1959.

Four years after Susan was born, they bought a three-bedroom home at 871 Moana Drive in La Jolla.

Susan said Jean was active in volunteer activities. "Mom was President of the PTA at Sunset View Elementary, and she belonged to the Junior League."

The Junior League is a service organization that helps young women serve the community. "It gives them the opportunity to develop their skills, supporting the community," Susan said.

Jean was supportive of her children's activities, Susan said. "When I was doing chorus at school, she was always helping us with our homework."

A journalism graduate from the University of California at Berkeley, Jean was very strict on grammar, Susan said. "Even into adulthood, she would correct us. In terms of usage, me versus I, lay versus lie, all that kind of stuff."

From 1968 until 1974, the Nicols lived in Sacramento, where Frank worked for the Reagan administration, as Deputy Director of California State Parks, then Director of the California Veteran's Administration.

Susan recalled the difficulties of moving to a new town at age 13: "I felt like I didn't have friends. I wasn't good at making friends, and I never had to make friends before. I had been through school with all the same people."

Four years later, when she was in high school in Sacramento, Frank raised the subject of moving back to San Diego.

"I was so upset, I jumped up and left the dinner table. I had made friends. I was in choirs and school. I think I had already been in a musical," she said. "I was quite dramatic about it."

Susan doesn't know if her outburst resulted in the family staying in Sacramento, but they did, for Reagan's second term as governor.

Her mother, Susan said, initially thought it was exciting to be involved in state politics, "but eventually, she was not all that impressed with many of the political people. There were some who were good friends and stayed good friends for a long time. But many of them, not so much."

Busy raising her three children while supporting her husband's career, Jean had no opportunity to pursue her own professional career, Susan said.

"I think Dad did not want her to work," Susan said. "He didn't think that was appropriate or necessary. It was the fifties. I think she felt cheated. The late sixties were the beginning of 'women's liberation.' I think she thinks she missed out."

At the end of Reagan's term as governor, the Nicol family returned to San Diego, where Frank resumed his insurance career. They remained there until they moved to Pauma Valley. Frank commuted daily to San Diego before retiring a few years later.

Jean contracted with Sim Bruce Richards, a protégé of renowned architect Frank Lloyd Wright, to build a custom home within the Pauma Valley Country Club.

"I think her self-fulfillment ultimately came from doing the research involved in choosing the property in Pauma Valley," Susan said. "To buy and build a house on it. She acted pretty much as the general contractor for building the house. She worked with an architect. It was an artistic and financial project that was her baby."[5]

Their home, built on a hillside with a view of the valley, was constructed with large glass windows that allow copious light into the home while offering a panoramic view of hills across the valley. The area is populated with numerous avocado groves and is located near Palomar Mountain.

"Mom did a lot of research on the water availability in Pauma Valley and the avocado market," Susan said.

Jean devoted some of her time researching the genealogy of the Nicol and Elliott families. She conducted much of her research in the 1980s, before the arrival of the internet, so Jean wrote numerous letters in her quest.

In the summer of 1976, Susan and Jean traveled to Homberg, Germany to research the Hund family. In the early 2000's, she and Jean took a trip to Scotland, where they visited libraries in Edinburgh to conduct family research.

In 1992, the Nicols began planting avocados on their 15-acre property. By 2000, the avocado trees began to produce a cash crop.

The nearby country club offered a golf course, tennis courts, pool, and a restaurant. Frank and Jean joined the club and developed numerous friendships in Pauma Valley.

Frank "loved to have parties and go to parties," Susan said. "And that was a burden on Mom. I think she felt that was just a lot of work for her. How much of that was the beginning of Alzheimer's, it's hard to know."

Susan said Frank and her brother, Todd, first noticed the Alzheimer's in the early 2000s. "She would forget things. Put Tupperware in the oven. And not take care of things she used to take care of," Susan said.

By 2006, Susan said, Jean was "certainly compromised cognitively. I remember in 2007 or 2008 I flew over on a Friday night. She waited up for me, and we talked in the living room. And it became clear she really didn't know who I was.

"She said, so where are you living these days? I said I'm still in Tucson, still working at Raytheon. She said, my daughter lives in Tucson," Susan recalled.

"Of course, I pivoted and said, yeah, I know her," Susan said. "She's doing really great. She's a great person. I think she said, you know, she divorced her husband. I said, yeah, I did hear that."

Susan said Jean's condition was very difficult for both Jean and Frank. "She really didn't know who Dad was. She thought he was a cousin. She was worried he was going to take her home."

In July 2009, Jean's condition took a turn for the worse when she fell in the kitchen and broke her hip. When she returned home five weeks later, she had to use a cane or walker to move around and was confined to the living room, to avoid using the stairs.

Throughout her life, Jean loved dogs. Toward the end, she was comforted by her dog Murphy, who was preceded by Midnight, Shadow, and several other dogs. Murphy usually lay by her side on the living room couch.

In a letter to his insurance company on 4 November 2009, Frank wrote that Jean had no recollection of her accident.

"Jean does not recall the names of relatives or friends, cannot handle phone calls, does not recall the names of our towns," Frank wrote, requesting medical care for Jean.[6]

I met Jean in a hospice home in Escondido a few months before she died. She had several newspapers lying on the couch, and she asked me about the latest news in the local paper. Despite her fragile state, Jean was still interested in journalism. I wish I could have told her I also had been a reporter at the Voice of America, but it was clear that Alzheimer's had erased her ability to make such connections.

In 2012, Jean passed away after suffering from Alzheimer's for several years. During that time, Frank took care of her and assumed household duties.

Todd lived nearby and helped Frank manage the grove. Alan and Susan traveled periodically from Washington state and Arizona. Alan performed crucial household repairs and maintenance. Susan helped with bookkeeping and taxes.

Frank passed away in 2015.

Several years after Frank died, Susan, Todd and Alan walked to the center of the bridge over the Stanislaus River at Board's Crossing and scattered the ashes of Frank and Jean over the water.

Jean's brother, John Jerome Elliott, played football at Long Beach Polytechnic High School. After graduating, he enrolled at the University of California at Berkeley (Cal). According to his World War II draft card, he was 6-foot-1, 195 pounds at age 19, with blue eyes and blond hair.

In Jean's letter for John's eulogy, she wrote that his college "was interrupted by the War when he served in the Navy" at the end of World War II. Unfortunately for John, "he had served ten days less than a year and was discharged. Those ten days made him eligible for the draft when Korea came around. And so he was off to the Army this time."

Jean said John's draft for the Korean War wasn't all bad because "He did, after all, get assigned to Redstone Arsenal, Alabama, where he learned to sail in that land of lakes and rivers."

After World War II, John returned to Cal and graduated. John married Emily (Sunny) Jones in 1960. An article in the *Star-News* of Pasadena said the couple planned a honeymoon in Palm Springs, to be followed by a trip "to Acapulco, then to Bermuda, and finally cruise with friends in the Mediterranean."[7]

They had two children, Blair, born in 1968, and Kent in 1970. John and Sunny lived in Corona del Mar, where John was an Orange County real estate developer. John passed away on 24 September 2001.

John Jerome Elliott, 1946
(Photo from Nicol Archives)

Sunny, John, Blair, Kent Elliott, 1982
(Photo from Nicol Archives)

10

Raymond Elliott

Raymond Davis Elliott, Jean's father, was born on 9 April 1886 in Rose Township, Carroll County, Ohio. He was the son of John M. Elliott and Margaret Agnes Davis.[1] His father, also born in Ohio, was a farmer.

In a 1980 letter to Jean Elliott Nicol from a cousin, Esther Elliott Whitmer, Esther recalled Margaret's recollections of Raymond:

"I do remember her talking about how he loved to read. She told of an incident that occurred one spring day when Raymond had the team of horses and was plowing up on the hillside above the old house. She said he decided to rest and read. He became absorbed in his book and the team of horses ran away."[2]

At the University of Chicago, Elliott was a member of the football team. He was listed as Left Guard in a souvenir catalogue of a 14 November 1908 Cornell-Chicago football game. The caption under his photo said Elliott was "one of the lightest and gamest guards playing football today."[3]

The line-up for the Chicago team, listed in the souvenir book, showed the average weight of a lineman at 172 pounds, and the average weight of the backfield was 169 pounds. The average Cornell player was 178 pounds. Elliott weighed 162. The game was a 6-6 tie; Chicago won its other five games that season.

The Chicago team held its own "by securing a tie with the brilliant Cornellians after they had at least held their own if not outplayed their rivals," a reporter from *The Inter Ocean* wrote.[4]

During an interview with the *Chicago Tribune* after the game, Chicago Coach Amos Alonzo Stagg said, "I consider the spirt shown by our boys to have been one of the best examples of spirit I have ever seen. They simply would not give in. They felt that the game belonged to them and fought as if they must have it."[5]

The souvenir book for the Chicago-Cornell game had numerous ads, including one for "The Arthur Imported $2.00 Hat" at 183 Dearborn St. An ad for the "Star and Garter" theater featured "Censored Burlesque" and "Rag-time Piano Playing Contests."

The book also ran an ad for "Chicago's Finest Automobile Livery," featuring "The World Famous Thomas Flyer Automobiles."

Raymond David Elliott, 1908
(Photo from University of Chicago Archives)

After graduating from the University of Chicago with a Bachelor of Science degree in 1909, Elliott coached a championship high school football team in Central, Ohio and another in Freemont, Ohio.[6]

In 1912, Elliott moved to Long Beach, California, where he taught chemistry and coached football at Long Beach

Polytechnic High School until 1916, when he went to the University of California at Berkeley to work on his master's degree in chemistry.

Elliott was a very competent football coach who helped University of California Golden Bears coach Andy Smith develop the team "into one of the outstanding football teams in the nation," according to an obit in *The Orange County Evening News* in 1971.[7]

A 1916 article in the *Long Beach Press-Telegram* said that while assisting the Golden Bears coach, "Elliott is the man who has prepared the way for a football victory over Washington next year by developing of freshman material. He modestly says that he deserves no credit, as the material he had to work on was the best he ever trained."[8]

After receiving his master's, Elliott joined Standard Oil and worked at its testing laboratory in Whittier. He invented oil field equipment and processes and subsequently headed up his own companies, Oilfields Service Co. and Geoanalyzer Corporation in Long Beach.

On his World War I draft card on 12 September 1918, Elliott listed his address as Whittier, Los Angeles County. The card noted that he was tall, with blue eyes and a "stout" build.[9] The war ended two months later, and he was not drafted.

Elliott, according to a 1921 article in *The Whittier News*, was a member of the Whittier Male Chorus.

"Many communities have their bands, orchestras, baseball teams, etc.," the article said, "but few have any organizations corresponding to the Whittier Male Chorus, which is composed of two dozen of the leading businessmen of this city."

The article said World War I had demonstrated that singing "serves to keep up the morale of an army and to create enthusiasm, and what is true in time of war is to a certain extent true in time of peace."

Raymond D. Elliott was one of six men named as Bass singers in the chorus.[10] A 1925 article in *The Whittier News* said Elliott sang "Oh Promise Me," at the wedding of a friend, Hal Will Smith, who was also a member of the Whittier chorus.[11]

Raymond Davis Elliott, 1909
(Photo from Nicol Archives)

On 7 October 1922, Elliott married Mary Lou Sherrill, who had moved from Greenville, Texas to Los Angeles. She was born in Greenville on 2 November 1888. In the 1910 U.S.

Census, Mary Lou was still living in Greenville, where she listed her occupation as "teaching in city schools."[12]

A 1907 yearbook for North Texas State Normal College at Denton lists Mary Lou Sherrill as a student.[13]

In the 1920 U.S. Census, Mary Lou was living at 409 South Grand Avenue, Los Angeles. At age 31, she listed her occupation as "stenographer" in the "pataphone" industry. The pataphone was a record player.[14]

Mary Lou Sherrill, age 21
(Photo from Nicol Archives)

Mary Lou's brother, James Dudley Sherrill, lived close by, at 419 S. Grand Ave., Los Angeles, according to his 1918 World War I draft card. James was born on 10 November 1899.[15] He listed his occupation as student.

James apparently died from drowning in the ocean at Del Mar, San Diego in July 1920. According to the Veteran's Administration, James had military service during World War I, although no records were found of his service.[16]

It's unclear when Raymond and Mary Lou met, but their daughter, Jean was born in Whittier on 21 December 1923. An article in the *Long Beach Press-Telegram* said Elliot and his family had lived in Long Beach since 1925. The article said Elliott was the Pacific Coast licensee for "Penetron" service, an electronic process for the measurement of pressure to be withstood by steel pipes and other metal receptacles.[17]

City records from 1930 show Raymond living at 2200 Eucalyptus Avenue, Long Beach.

Susan Nicol Thibodeaux, his granddaughter, recalled having dinner with Raymond and Mary Lou in their home on several occasions in the 1960s, when they lived in Garden Grove. As a young child, Susan called Mary Lou "Gong Gong," a name that stuck with her grandchildren years later. Raymond was "Pop," although he was known as "Pat" to his friends.

While living in Long Beach, Elliott was appointed to the Long Beach Harbor Commission, where he served for two and a half years. He was also director of the Long Beach Chamber of Commerce, working as a member of its oil committee.

Elliott was active in civic affairs. In 1942, During World War II, he attended the Chemical Warfare School of Civilian

Protection at Stanford University, at his own expense. He then became an Air Raid Warden instructor in Long Beach.[18]

Elliott moved to Garden Grove in 1950 and became a real estate developer. He first visited Garden Grove in 1921 to drill a test hole for Standard Oil.

"It was a deep hole and we didn't get much out of it," he told a reporter. "But I liked the area so much I determined that here was where I would someday build my home."[19]

In 1952, Elliott and a partner, William Farrow, built Garden Square, the first shopping center in Orange County. They also created some of the early sub-divisions of Garden Grove, including "Sunny Acres" at Garden Grove Blvd. and Newhope Street.

Elliott was a member of the Garden Grove Chamber of Commerce. In 1958, he was appointed foreman of the Orange County Grand Jury.

He passed away on 18 February 1971. Mary Lou died on 19 August 1972.

Raymond's father, John M. Elliott, was born on 3 August 1860 in Rose Township, Carroll County, Ohio. In the 1880 U.S. Census, he identified himself as a farmer, living in Monroe township, Carroll County.

On 11 October 1883, John married Margaret Agnes Davis, who was born on 06 February 1858 in Monroe. In the 1900 U.S. Census, John and Margaret listed four children: Raymond, 14, Loren, 10, Winona, 8, and Paul, 5. He owned his farm and home, free of mortgage.[20]

John Elliott lived and worked on his farm until he died on 29 May 1931.

**John Elliott, date unknown
(Photo from Nicol Archives)**

John Elliott was the son of James Blaine Elliott, who was born on 20 January 1832 in Rose Township, Carroll County. John's mother was Mary Wilson, who was born on 22 May 1829 in Carroll County.

Like his son, John, James Elliott was also a farmer. In the 1870 U.S. Census, his home was still in Rose Township, Carroll County, Ohio. He was apparently a prosperous farmer, since his real estate was valued at $14,000 and his personal estate at $2,500—both substantial sums for that time.[21]

According to Carroll County Veteran Grave Registration records, James Elliott served in the Union Army during the Civil War. The record gives his correct name, date of birth, and date of death; however, it does not list his rank or unit. The record said that he died of cancer in 1897.[22]

National Archive records list more than a dozen men from Ohio named James Elliott who served in the Civil War, but only one James B. Elliott, who was ten years younger and died in combat. The Carroll County grave registration records are the only evidence available on Elliott's Civil War service, but the lack of National Archive records does not mean that he did not serve. Those records are often incomplete.

James Elliott died on 09 March 1897 in Carroll County; his wife, Mary, died there on 11 March 1917.

On his 1880 U.S. Census form, James Elliott said his father was born in Ireland and his mother in Pennsylvania.

Aaron Elliot, his father, was born in May 1792 in Donegal, Ireland, according to the *U.S. Find A Grave Index*.[23] Donegal County, part of the Republic of Ireland, forms a land border with three Northern Ireland counties.

Just when Aaron arrived in America is uncertain, but Jean Elliott Nicol conducted extensive correspondence with several Elliott relatives in Ohio who believe that Aaron's parents, George Elliott and Isabella Blaine, decided to leave Ireland in 1799 and emigrate to America. That date corresponds with later census records, immigration records and tax rolls for Aaron Elliott..

Their decision to leave Ireland was serendipitous, since the Irish Rebellion of 1798 saw nearly 30,000 people lose their lives amid warfare between Catholics and Protestants. The Elliotts were Presbyterian. Ireland was also suffering from a poor economy and drought, and immigrants to America sent back glowing reports of opportunities in America.

George Elliott apparently died of unknown causes just before their departure in 1799, and Isabella embarked on a voyage to America with as many as ten children, of whom two died during the eleven-week voyage. No immigration records for Isabella Blaine Elliott could be found, but she apparently made her way to Pennsylvania. She was likely helped by friends and relatives who had already emigrated from Ireland.

The older children were apparently farmed out to Presbyterian missionaries, and Aaron Elliot was one of these. He would have been about eight or nine years old. Since his future wife, Jane Miller, was born in Washington County, Pennsylvania in 1797, it is likely that Aaron either lived with her family or was a neighbor.

Aaron Elliott and Jane Miller were married on 2 January 1821 in Washington County and moved to Carroll County, Ohio. On the marriage record, Elliott listed his year of birth as 1792, in Ireland. Their first son, George Elliott, was born in Ohio on 04 March 1822.[24]

Elliott is listed as a resident of Rose Township, Stark County, Ohio in the 1830 U.S. Census. Carroll County was formed from parts of Stark County in 1833. In 1834, Elliott was listed on the tax rolls of Rose Township in Carroll County.[25]

In 1835, Elliott was naturalized as a U.S. citizen.[26] On the 1850 U.S. Census record, Elliott said his birthplace was Ireland and his occupation farmer. He said his real estate was valued at $3,500, and he listed eight children.

His oldest, George, gave his occupation as physician. George also listed his occupation as physician on his U.S. Civil War Draft Registration Record.

In 1850, Aaron Elliott signed an affidavit stating that he served as a soldier during the War of 1812, when America fought the British the second time. Elliott said he enlisted as a private in the 1st Infantry Regiment of the Virginia militia, under Capt. John Elson, from September 1812 through April 1813.

His affidavit was in support of a request for a Land Bounty offered to veterans. His application was later rejected. A National Archives records search on Elliott requested by Jean Elliott Nicol in 1979 produced no records of military service for Aaron; however, the absence of records does not mean Elliott did not serve. Records for that period were sometimes missing or not forwarded to the National Archives.

Given the plethora of names and dates that Elliott provided on his application, it is likely that he did serve in the war.

Aaron Elliott was among the founders of the Big Springs Presbyterian Church in Carroll County. He died at age 63 on 21 August 1855 in Carroll County, followed by his wife, Jane, on 02 May 1857.

11

Sherrill

Mary Lou Sherrill, who married Raymond D. Elliott in Los Angeles in 1922, was the daughter of James Stevens Sherrill and Katherine Crossland Farr of Greenville, Texas.

Born on 2 November 1888, she was one of six children born to James and Katherine.

In 1888, Greenville, in Hunt County, produced high quality cotton, which brought in railroads and prosperity. It was home to Audie Murphy, a sharecropper's son who became the most decorated soldier of World War II.

Mary Lou's father, James Stevens Sherrill was born on 15 September 1854 in Fannin County, Texas, which is just north of Greenville. It was named for James Fannin, who commanded a group of Texans killed in the Goliad Massacre during the Texas Revolution.

**Mary Lou Sherrill, circa 1904
(Photo from Nicol Archives)**

The Fannin county seat of Bonham is located about fifty-five miles north of Dallas.

The early settlers of Fannin County in the late 1830s "faced many difficulties with Indians, particularly with the Cherokees and their Twelve Associated Bands," according to the Texas State Historical Association.

Tensions had been mounting as the Indians grew less friendly with the influx of white settlers and the resulting damage to hunting.

"The Indians retaliated with constant raids of their own in which settlers were killed and livestock stolen. Residents of Fannin County were infuriated particularly by Indians' practice of mutilating dead bodies, and their indiscriminate killing of women and children."[1]

Most of the early settlers were from the South, particularly Tennessee, the home of Byrd Thaddeus Sherrill, the father of James. By the time Byrd arrived in Texas in 1850, tensions had eased with the Indians. Texas became a republic after gaining its independence from Mexico in 1836, and it joined the Union in 1845.

Sewantly (Sarah) Stevens, the mother of James Sherrill, was born in Lawrence, Alabama. She moved to Fannin County with her parents and married Byrd Sherrill about 1853. A marriage certificate for Byrd and Sarah could not be located, but the 1931 Texas death certificate of their son, James, lists Sewantly Stevens as his mother and Byrd Sherrill as his father.[2]

The Sherrill family settled on a farm near the county seat of Bonham.

A 1909 article in the *Honey Grove Signal* said Fannin County was "a fine grazing country; cattle and horses could live all winter without have to be fed. Grass was abundant everywhere. Hogs that ran loose in the belts of timber kept fat on the mast, acorns and pecans being abundant." [3]

James Sherrill attended public schools in Bonham. According to an article in the *Greenville Evening Banner,* "As a young man he taught school and afterwards attended Bonham Christian College."[4]

In 1877, James married Leola Hall. They had a child, Cleo Sherrill, born in July 1878. Sherrill was admitted to the state bar in 1878, after studying the law under a local judge in Bonham, where he graduated from Carlton College.

Leola died in 1881, at age 28. The cause of her death is unknown. On 12 January 1883, Sherrill married Kate Crossland Farr.

Sherrill, a Democrat, was elected judge in Greenville in 1884. He served in the Texas House of Representatives from

January 1893 to January 1895 for Hunt County, and in the Texas Senate from January 1895 to Jan 1897. He returned to the House in January 1899, when he was elected Speaker.

"He was considered one of the most powerful and influential legislators in the state," according to an obituary in the *Greenville Evening Banner*.[5]

While Sherrill presided as speaker, according to the *Banner*, "the legislature added to its system of state colleges an institution for higher education in Denton that eventually became the University of North Texas."

After his term as Speaker, Sherrill resumed his law practice in Greenville. He is listed as a resident of Greenville in the 1900 and 1910 U.S. Census reports, as well as the 1916 city directory.

In the 1920 Census, he was a resident of Houston, at 3006 Smith St. According to the Census data, he owned his home, free of mortgage.[6]

Sherrill moved to Houston to work as an attorney for the Federal Land Bank. According to the University of Texas, the federal land bank system was created in 1916, which established a cooperative association for low-interest credit to farmers.

He died in Houston in 1931, at age 76.

James Stevens Sherrill
(Legislative Reference Library of Texas)

James Stevens Sherrill's father, Byrd Thaddeus Sherrill, was born in Tennessee in 1815. By age 25, he was living in Mississippi.

Byrd was listed as County Treasurer for Tunica County, Mississippi from 1840 to 1844.[7]

Byrd's first wife, Elenor Phillips, married Byrd on 25 September 1845 and died in 1850 of unknown causes.

In the 1850 U.S. Census, Byrd, 35, was still residing in Tunica County, Mississippi. He listed his occupation as farmer and his birthplace as Tennessee.[8]

He moved to Fannin County, Texas about 1850, likely following the death of Elenor. After arriving in Texas, Byrd married Sewantly (Sarah) Stevens—the mother of James Stevens Sherrill. Since their first son, James, was born in 1854, it is likely they were married about 1853.

Sewantly died on 21 January 1860, after giving birth to five children.

The identity of Byrd Sherrill's father remains an enigma. Numerous genealogical sites identity him as Jesse Sherrill, but evidence for that connection is missing.

Jesse Sherrill was listed as a resident of Roane County, Tennessee in the 1805 Tennessee Census records.[9] Several census and marriage records list him as residing in Tennessee, but no record of a son, Byrd, could be found.

On his 1850 U.S. Census declaration, Byrd Sherrill says his father was born in Virginia—not Tennessee.

It is likely that Byrd Sherrill was descended from a branch of the family of William Sherrill, who was born in Devon, England on 16 November 1666. He emigrated to America at age 20 and settled in Cecil County, Maryland, where he died in 1747.

His son, the first Adam Sherrill born in America in 1696, headed for North Carolina after his father died, along with his brother, William Sherrill. They settled on the west side of the Catawba River, then later moved on to Tennessee. Eastern Tennessee was on the migration path of many Americans moving west after the Revolutionary War.

Two Sherrills, Adam—the son of Adam or William—and Adam's father, Samuel, fought as soldiers in the Revolutionary Army during America's war for independence.

Adam fought in the Battle of King's Mountain in South Carolina on 07 October 1780. The battle was a fierce fight in which loyalist soldiers under command of British officers attempted to gain control of the Southern colonies.

The American patriots won a decisive victory over the British. It was a turning point in the war, boosting American morale, badly needed following the capture of Charleston by the British, led by General Cornwallis. The victory forced Cornwallis to abandon his plans to invade North Carolina. It was the first of a series of setbacks that led to the defeat of the British in America.

Only two months later, on 16 December 1780, Adam Sherrill fought at the Battle of Boyd's Creek in Tennessee, when soldiers from East Tennessee, Virginia and North Carolina defeated a large force of Cherokee Indians who had been attacking settlers.

The Cherokees were allies of the British, who had encouraged the Cherokees to attack white settlements. The homes of many of the militiamen fighting at the Battle of King's Mountain were attacked while the men were away fighting.

Adam Sherrill was joined at the Battle of King's Mountain by his father, Samuel Sherrill, who was born on 01 October 1725 in Cecil County, Maryland. Samuel moved from Maryland to Virginia, then to North Carolina and Tennessee.

Since Sherrill was not a common name during that time, it is highly likely that Byrd Sherrill was a descendant of Adam or Samuel.

12

Farr

Katherine Crossland Farr, the future wife of James Stevens Sherrill, was born on 10 October 1860 in Greenville, Hunt County, Texas.

Greenville was incorporated as a town only eight years earlier, but it already boasted a general merchandise store, three taverns, three grocery stores, two hotels and a drug store.

In 1860, on the eve of the Civil War, Hunt County voted to join the Confederacy, and Greenville raised a company of soldiers who saw action in Arkansas and Tennessee.

Katherine's father, James Farr, was one of those soldiers. He was a captain in the Confederate Army and served as a quartermaster officer in Louisiana.[1]

In a letter to Confederate commanders in Shreveport, Louisiana, dated 01 October 1864, Farr requested release from duty in his battalion. He said he had served as quartermaster for the Stevens Regiment of Texas Calvary from 01 July 1862 to 01 March 1864, but was "dismounted" and assigned to a battalion. He requested reassignment to a regiment or brigade.

"I was in Texas only a few years before the war," he wrote. "I was in practice of the law in my town and had received license from the Supreme Court of our State."

A reply from Confederate command to his letter, dated 19 August 1864 said, "In accordance with the decision of Department Headquarters not allowing a quartermaster to a battalion, Capt. Farr is hereby relieved from duty with the same and ordered to report to Col. J.E. Harrison, 2nd Brigade commander, Sicily Island, Louisiana."

The exchange of letters between Farr and the Confederate command in Louisiana are included in his file with the National Archives. His complaint essentially was that he had been transferred to a command that was beneath his rank.

The value of these letters lies in establishing his time of arrival in Texas and his own validation of his status as an attorney in the state. Based on this letter from Farr, it is likely he arrived in Hunt County in 1857 or 1858. He apparently traveled alone to Texas and managed to get an education as a lawyer by age 25.

Farr was born on 24 July 1834 in Hickman, Fulton County, Kentucky. On the 1850 U.S. Census, he was listed as a farmer in Hickman, at age 16.[2] His father, Robert King Farr, died when James was only a year old.

His mother remarried in 1856 to John Motheral. Since Farr arrived in Texas a year or two later, that marriage may have been the impetus for his departure from Kentucky.

By 1860, Census records note that he was a lawyer, living in Greenville, Hunt County, Texas.[3]

James Farr, like many attorneys of his era, likely studied the law under the tutelage of a licensed attorney in Texas. Several articles refer to him as an attorney, but records from that time are scarce. He is listed as an attorney on the 1880 U.S. Census.

In 1859, Farr married Laurena Finney Stevens, who was born on 14 November 1829 in Alabama.[4] She had moved to Texas with her parents, Lewis and Sarah Finney Stevens.

According to the 1850 U.S. Census for Fannin, Texas, Laurena Stevens had a sister named "S. Stevens," whose parents, Lewis Stevens and Sarah Finney, were from Alabama.

It appears very likely that Sewantly "Sarah" Stevens, who was the mother of James Stevens Sherrill, was the sister of Laurena Stevens. The census records also listed Lewis Stevens and Sarah Finney as the parents of Sarah.

James and Laurena Farr had six children, of whom at least one, Louis Lee Farr, was very successful.

A brief notice in the *El Paso Times* on 05 May 1900 says, "Capt. James Farr, a pioneer citizen and father of Louis L. Farr, mayor of San Angelo, died Wednesday."

In addition to his position as mayor of San Angelo, Louis Farr was a rancher, banker and county surveyor. He was twice elected county tax assessor and subsequently established the Fort Concho Realty Company. Farr was vice-president of the Central National Bank in San Angelo and was business manager for the Yates oilfield.[5]

**James Farr headstone, San Angelo, TX
(Photo courtesy of U.S. Find A Grave Index)**

Epilogue

Susan, Todd and Alan Nicol now spend summers at the Nicol home at Board's Crossing. The place requires a great deal of maintenance but offers a wonderful opportunity to escape the outside world.

Amid the solitude of the mountains, the Stanislaus River flows wider in front of the Nicol home, offering a place to swim and paddle around on kayaks or boats. In the afternoon, the descending sun creates a soft light that transforms the river into a kaleidoscope of colors and shadows.

One can sit on the balcony of the guest house or on a chair at the sandy beach and contemplate the beauty of nature. Giant ponderosa and sugar pine trees loom over the houses.

Sometimes an eagle or osprey will fly along the river, searching for a trout, or a flock of geese will swim up to the landing looking for insects. At night the occasional fox may wander across the place, and sometimes, a black bear will stop by in search of food.

It is a place where weekend guests come to socialize with the Nicols. There is no television and no need for one. People talk, read, eat and share bottles of wine.

Board's Crossing is a special place, a repository of memories of the past and of those being made.

Interview with Irene Hund

On 15 June 1980, Jean Elliott Nicol conducted an interview with Irene Hund Nicol, who was Frank Nicol's mother. Irene was the daughter of Frederick and Carrie Hund.

In her files, Jean, now deceased, left a transcript of her interview with Irene.

Following is a transcript of the interview:

JEAN: What do you remember about growing up?

IRENE: Everybody but me was grown up.

JEAN: You were the bratty little sister?

IRENE: I was the sensitive one who had to adjust to everybody else.

JEAN: Why was that?

IRENE: Everybody was grown up but me. Our whole life was blasted by the earthquake. Everything was very lovely and very prosperous before the earthquake. My grandmother used to say the hardest reputation to live down was that you were rich. Then the earthquake came and just pulled the rug out from everything.

I was sharing a bed with Selma (Berndt, a cousin), when all the stuff fell over our bed. I remember Papa saying, come here and stand under the doors. My brother Fred came flying down. He had had a hemorrhage before then and was supposed to be absolutely quiet in bed. You could hear him screaming down the stairs. My whole bed was full of dishes, because I had this cabinet next to the bed, with all kinds of lovely dishes.

JEAN: Why was Selma staying with you?

IRENE: Easter vacation. Selma used to come over and spend vacations with me. Her mother was a Meussdorffer. I remember on Good Friday we went to church. We rode the horse down. My mother had given us a nickel or dime to put in the collection plate. Much to our great delight, they didn't pass the plate, and we went to the store and blew it on some candy.

JEAN: You were living in Ross then?

IRENE: Yeah. Everything that Grandpa had was lost (in San Francisco). In those days people didn't invest in stocks and bonds. If you had some extra money to invest, it was always real estate. We had nine income properties south of Market. The earthquake knocked them all down and burned then all up. And no insurance—the insurance companies all went broke. My father's medical instruments were all burned up, his books, everything.

I always remember sitting out in the grove the night after the earthquake. Wallie and Erwin were over at Berkeley. Grandpa sat there in the dark and said, It's all gone, everything we have is gone. The city's doomed. We were afraid to go back in the house, so we sat out in the grove. We sat there in the dark, and he said, it's all gone. But he said if the boys get home everything will be all right. About ten o'clock that night, we heard a whistle, out in the road. And he said, there they are. They got a launch that took them over to Sausalito.

My father had to start in all over again. He started his office in San Rafael. And he had all these boys who were college age. I don't know how he did it. About 1909 he sent the two to Europe (Walter and Fred) to get their graduate work in chemistry, and Harry and Erwin to Philadelphia to finish their medical studies.

After the earthquake Wally and Fred worked on disaster relief in San Francisco for quite a while, handing out shoes and clothes.

JEAN: How old were you, compared to the boys?

IRENE: I was six years younger than the youngest boy.

JEAN: Where was it you lived?

IRENE: We lived on Laurel Grove Avenue in Ross. We had the first telephone of that street. Everyone used to come to our place to phone. In 1907 we built the sanitarium. Before the earthquake my father had been practicing in San Francisco and commuted back and forth on the ferry. In San Francisco he had a buggy and a driver that took him around to make his calls. About 1907 my father bought his first car, a Maxwell. I drove the car when I was about 11.

JEAN: Where did you drive?

IRENE: I'd just drive around Ross. They used to have signs that said, "automobiles prohibited." I had a driver's license that said, "good until revoked."

JEAN: Before that, you had horses?

IRENE: Of course, we always had horses. They used to take us down to the train (Northwestern Pacific) in Ross. It was about a mile. The gardener was also the driver, and he took care of the horses, too. My father and the boys who were working in San Francisco used to take the 6:40 train every morning to catch the ferry.

JEAN: Where was Meta when you were born?

IRENE: Meta Steffen was there in the house when I was born, so I don't know where she came from. Mama needed some help with all those boys in the house and put out the word that she was looking for someone. Meta applied, and at first mama said Meta was too young—only 15 or 16 years old. But she was hired and was always a part of the whole family. Meta's father came from Chicago.

JEAN: What about food? Did you have a garden?

IRENE: I don't know that was ever a problem. I was going to Miss Stewart's school in San Rafael. I used to go to dancing school at the Lagunitas Country Club. I rode a horse to school every day, over the hill to San Rafael.

JEAN: Do you remember living in San Francisco?

IRENE: No, I don't remember that. I was born in San Francisco, but I don't remember living there. I'm not sure when they built the Ross house. My mother's cousin, Conrad

Meussdorffer, was the architect both of our homes, and later the sanitarium.

Laurel Grove Avenue was a beautiful place—a succession of lovely homes and gardens. A wonderful climate. The house had three floors. The middle floor was the company floor, with living and dining room, Papa's library, what had been a music room but was turned into a billiard room. The bottom floor was the everyday floor. Upstairs were the bedrooms.

When I was about 9 years old, I was sent to a girl's school because I didn't know how to play with girls. I grieved, and said if I couldn't play with the boys, couldn't I sit on the fence and watch them? I didn't enjoy the school much, but I made some good friends. Elizabeth Kent, Mary Armsby, Marian Christensen. We had this little group we Called the "Literary Lump." We spent overnights and weekends at each other's homes. We all had horses, and wherever we were invited, our horses were invited too.

JEAN: You had dances?

IRENE: We had monthly dances—we called them "hops"— with the two military academies in San Rafael. This was when we were from 10 to 14 or 16 years old. Of course, we had chaperones.

JEAN: Who were the chaperones?

IRENE: Your mother would go and sit there with you. I had a party once before a dance at the Lagunitas Club. It was when ragtime first came out—it was considered very daring. "The Grizzly Bear," that song Susan (Irene's granddaughter) likes, came out then. I had the sheet music, and someone dared put it on the piano—we thought we were very devilish.

JEAN: Do you remember when your mother and father bought the property at Freestone?

IRENE: My mother and father (Frederick J. Hund and Caroline Zech Hund) bought the Freestone property about 1910 or 1911. Wallie and Fred were in school in Germany, taking their post graduate work in chemistry, and they became interested in growing and manufacturing drugs. They were looking for a place with lots of water, and that's when they found the acreage.

JEAN: What kind of drugs?

 IRENE: The drugs they were interested in growing were digitalis, mint, and maybe belladonna. With their chemistry background they planned to manufacture these drugs, but they found they couldn't produce enough to make it pay. During that time is when they went up there and lived in the house. Will Grass was with them. Will was thinking about getting married then, and that's when they started the house. It was designed from a drawing Wallie had made of a Swiss chalet he had seen in Europe.

JEAN: The railroad was there then?

IRENE: Oh yeah. The railroad that went past the house then was built about 1875. It went to San Anselmo, Fairfax, White's Hill tunnel and Pt. Reyes. The train stopped running in 1932, and they later took the trestle down. The stumps from the redwood trees in the meadow were gigantic. Those stumps took 30 sticks of dynamite to blast out (about 1952).

My mother and father moved to Freestone for good in the spring of 1921, after Lawrence and I were married.

Our lovely home—sanitarium, laboratory, four housing units, stable and garage plus six acres of gardens and seven plus acres of redwood grove and wooded hills sold to the catholic church for $35,000 in the spring of 1921.

Leading up to the wedding, Papa (Lawrence Nicol) and I met because he and Wallie met in France during WWI, one dark night in front of the Chateau in St. Anyan. They were the only Californians there—most of them were from the east. Wallie wrote home that he'd met a young man from San Francisco, and whose mother lived there, and suggested we invite her over to visit. We did, but she replied she was an invalid and would we come to see her. My mother and I went to see her (Adelaide Dodge Nicol). She showed us lots of pictures. Later, Lawrence went to the Sorbonne, and Wallie came home. When Lawrence came back, he came over to see Wallie. They had both been in the statistical division over there, and they shared an apartment. Later Wallie was transferred to the chemical warfare division because of his chemistry background. Lawrence came back, and he used to come over to see Wallie on weekends. He was eight years older than I am, and it never occurred to me that he would be my little playmate. I was in the Navy then, and on Monday he used to go back with me on the train.

Every weekend there was like Thanksgiving. All the young married would come for Sunday dinner. On Monday morning I would go to San Francisco to work, and we'd all go on the train together. One day, Lawrence told me he had my picture. I asked him where he had gotten it. He said Wallie had left it on the mantle in their apartment in France, and he kept it. He said he didn't want Wallie's sister's picture kicking all over France, so he brought it back.

JEAN: What were you doing in San Francisco then, Grandpa (Lawrence)?

IRENE: He wasn't doing anything, then. He was trying to figure things out.

JEAN: Before the war, you worked as an attorney for Goodfellow, Eels, and Orrick, in San Francisco. What kind of law was it?

LAWRENCE: Corporation law.

IRENE: Animals were a great part of my early life. I had no companions of my own age, but I had cats, dogs—the pigeons used to come to meet me coming from school—rabbits and chipmunks.

JEAN: Do you recall how many acres you had?

IRENE: Yes. We had fourteen acres. Before the earthquake we just had seven or eight acres, and then my father bought the additional acres from Dr. Wyle, and that's when we built the sanitarium.

JEAN: And your brothers built the house in Freestone?

IRENE: Yes, and my parents moved there full-time when my father retired. The house wasn't finished then. A fellow named Bartoldi came up and lived with them for a while and finished the house in 1921. They built the extra bedroom downstairs when my mother broke her leg, because she couldn't get up the stairs. (From an auto accident in 1928.)

JEAN: What was your relationship with Will Grass?

IRENE: Will Grass was my mother's cousin. Grandma's mother was Susanna Grass, who married Jacob Zech. One of

Susanna's sisters was Anna Caroline Zech, who married Meussdorffer in San Francisco. They had a couple of brothers—Uncle Pete, Uncle Frank and so on. Will was the son of one of those. The Meussdorffers had a hat business in San Francisco. Will Grass's brother Frank lived with them just like Will lived with us.

JEAN: I think it's important for your children and your great-grandchildren to know how things were. That's the reason I'm interested in this, from an historical viewpoint. How did we all get where we are, and why? What kind of people were they? How hard did they have to work? What kinds of things did they have to go through to get where we are now?

IRENE: I don't remember anything about my grandparents because they all died before I was born. Some of the relatives I do remember. They tell me I used to scream and yell every time Tante Koch (Appolonia Grass Koch, sister of Susanna Grass Zech) appeared because she was a kind of frightening looking person. She used to reach around the corner and hand me a cookie before she came in.

JEAN: Who was Appolonia Grass Koch?

IRENE: She was my grandmother's sister.

JEAN: Why did Will Grass come to live with you?

IRENE: Because his mother had one of these conditions where every time she had a baby she went nutty. Will went to live with my grandmother (Susanna Grass Zech). When my grandmother died, he had nowhere to go so they just put him in with the rest of the boys in our house.

JEAN: What do you recall about your father?

IRENE: My father (Frederick John Hund) was an excellent doctor. He was one of the first ones to do some of the very serious surgery taking out a part of a person's stomach and hooking it together again, instead of just letting him die. He did a lot of work along those lines. He was on the diagnostic staff at St. Luke's Hospital in San Francisco for a long time.

He used to work and work and work. He had a very well-stocked library and studied and read constantly. And then along came the earthquake, and all of momma's beautiful glassware and these beautiful oak cabinets. Everything was moved tightly against the doors. But not one of those doors flew open. So nothing went out. But in the library, Papa's books all ended up on the floor.

FRANK: Did your family ever go on vacations?

IRENE: I remember three camping trips we went on. All of us—my mother and father, the boys, Meta, Tante Tillie. The first year we went between Willits and Fort Bragg. This old lady, Mrs. Jones, and her brother had property in there. I guess they were patients of Papa's. We went up on the train, then took the stage and stayed there. There was a little stream, but no one had bathing suits. I was only six years old, so I put on a pair of pants. And Papa got gunny sacks and cut the corners out for the boys.

JEAN: How long did you stay there?

IRENE: We stayed six weeks or two months. Two years later we went to Potter Valley, which is out from Ukiah toward the Eel River. We camped there. Then, the last one was just the year before the earthquake. We went to Cazadero, then to Plantation House, and to an old ranch on the Gualala River owned by some people named Kase, which means cheese (in

German). We went swimming there. I remember riding bareback, without a saddle or bridle or anything. The horse would swim across the river, with me on it.

That's when the Schmidt's were camping with us. Max Schmidt had had a mental breakdown, and they wanted to be near my father. So the Schmidts and our boys started out early, took all the horses and tents and supplies up early. They stopped at Uncle Pete's and got a barrel of wine, and set up camp. Then my mother and father, Meta and I went up on the train. The boys set up the tents and built a trough from this beautiful spring. The Schmidt's kitchen was on one side of the trough, and ours was on the other. And that's when I learned all these songs from Ben Schmidt. I was nine years old.

JEAN: Was your whole family musical? You learned to play the piano?

IRENE: I always had music lessons, but I never liked the lessons and played things my own way. Herr Widder used to come over every weekend and give us lessons. He was an engineer, but he had this amazing talent for music. He organized all our big parties, when everyone played something. Mr. Widder and I never got along very well. First, because he always had unpleasant remarks about me being fat. And then he would show me how to play something and I would play it back, but in another key. He would swear at me in German. He finally figured I wanted to play something with more zip to it.

Susan and Todd Nicol

John Young interviewed Susan Nicol Thibodeaux and Todd Nicol on 28 September 2020 at the Nicol residence, Board's Crossing.

Following is a transcript of the interview:

JY: Where did you hear the story about Lawrence meeting Wally Hund in France during World War I?

TODD: My dad told me about it. They were both in the trenches. It was catastrophic. He said very little about this.

JY: So they were both on the front line, infantry?

TODD: Yeah.

JY: So, the American Army found they could speak German?

SUSAN: They were interrogators. That's what I heard. They needed German speaking people to do that. Now, to what extent Lawrence was fluent, I cannot say. My impression is, he had a rudimentary knowledge of German. Not like the Hunds did. Because the Hunds grew up speaking German. They learned German before they learned English. When the war started, they stopped speaking German altogether. I did want to comment on Irene. I remember Irene telling me she was always a fat lump. She did not feel good about herself physically.

TODD: And they were worried about her. The brother showed him the picture and promoted her. I think they started writing.

JY: After he got back, according to the 1920 census, Lawrence was still an attorney, but it appears later they moved out to Brentwood and bought a farm?

SUSAN: A ranch. We called it the almond ranch.

JY: How did Irene feel about living on the ranch after living in San Francisco?

SUSAN: I heard that she thought she was marrying a sophisticated San Francisco attorney. And then, all of a sudden, she's got to live in the middle of nowhere. Brentwood was pretty much in the middle of nowhere at that point. And she had three children relatively quickly. They were all in diapers at one point. She had no help on the ranch. She was exhausted.

JY: So you met Lawrence and Irene?

SUSAN: Sure. I don't remember talking to her at my wedding, but she was there. Lawrence had already died. (Lawrence died in 1984; Sue's wedding was 1987. Irene died in 1988.) I always felt that she was hanging on because she wanted to see me married.

JY: Did she talk to you about being overweight when she was a young woman?

SUSAN: I do remember her saying she was a fat lump.

TODD: When you're not beautiful, you develop yourself in other ways. She played music, and got the party going. She had a thousand songs that she could sing.

SUSAN: She wasn't a singer so much, but she could play the piano and banjo by ear. A lot of the turn of the 20th century songs. (Susan and Todd singing: "You made me love you. I didn't want to do it.")

TODD: We grew up listening to all those songs.

JY: Was that at Freestone?

SUSAN: Sometimes.

JY; Tell me about Freestone. Frederick Hund bought the property at Freestone and built the house?

SUSAN: That sounds right.

TODD: There was three women living there, and that was scandalous.

JY: As kids, you went up there?

SUSAN: We would get in the station wagon in San Diego and drive to northern California. When we lived in Sacramento we would get in the car and drive to southern California for vacations. Or come up here to Board's Crossing.

JY: What was Freestone like when you were kids? What did you do?

SUSAN: In addition to grandma playing the banjo—there was no piano there. Because they lived in Berkeley, in the Piedmont house. They figured out that during the war (WWII), unless they took boarders in, like college students, they were going to be housing ship-building workers. This was Irene and Lawrence. They finally sold the ranch. I'm going to say late fifties. And they bought the house at 2123 Piedmont avenue.

TODD: It was a magnificent house. I can remember being there when I was a little boy. And the women upstairs.

JY: So there were college students boarding there?

SUSAN: Women. Just women.

TODD: I can remember them running around in their towels. And that's also where I was when John Kennedy died.

SUSAN: You went up with mom and dad that weekend. I remember it because mom and dad were going to the big game, but it was canceled because of the assassination. My first plane flight was from San Diego to Oakland, to visit grandma and grandpa. I went by myself. Because all these coeds lived there, and they would move out at the end of the school year, they would leave random things behind. Nothing of particular value. One of the things we used to do at Freestone, with Elaine and Walter's children, they had this little thing they got in Chinatown, where you poked a little thing through and a paper came out and you had to do what it said, like do a headstand, or sing happy birthday, or whatever. Then, if you successfully did it, you got to pick from the no-touch box. There was this box, with all the things the girls left, and you got to pick something. They were just little things that had been left. It was great fun.

JY: So you had a good relationship with Irene and Lawrence?

TODD: Lawrence, he was a dude all to himself. He was not really communicative. He would sing with us at Ossy-bussy hour, but he was a very sparing in interactions.

SUSAN: To say we were close is not accurate.

JY: Was Irene more talkative?

TODD: Oh yes.

SUSAN: She was a lot of fun. So after they left Berkeley and the Piedmont house, they moved to Rossmoor in Walnut Creek. In the century he grew up in, California changed a lot. It used to be a wonderful place. By the sixties or seventies, things just weren't the way they used to be.

TODD: One of the problems with Lawrence was, he had an eye that went slightly in one direction.

SUSAN: I don't remember that.

JY: Todd, you said you thought that Lawrence's experience in war changed him. Your dad told you that?

TODD: I might have heard it from my mom. I don't think my dad would have told me that. He went to Hastings, and he was a lawyer. And he got put in the trenches. They called it shell shock. I remember a ton of different stories, of what life was like, at the ranch.

JY: My impression of your dad, Frank, was that he did not like living on the ranch. Am I correct?

SUSAN: It was hard work. And it was boring. By visiting Nicol Smith and his family, he had just a taste of what it was like to live in the city, and be with social people. He couldn't wait to go to college. He had to wait a year, though, because I don't think they had the money to send him to Berkeley.

JY: When Frank was at Cal-Berkeley, he was on the JV rowing team. He got to the national finals?

SUSAN: He desperately wanted to go to the national finals at Poughkeepsie, but he wasn't in the first boat. He somehow convinced his parents that it was okay for him to stowaway in the baggage car to cross country. They really didn't want him to go. They wanted him to come home and work on the ranch for the summer. And he was going to be gone all summer. Somehow that got negotiated. He just said I'm going. So he and someone else were going to stowaway, but then days before they were going to leave, one of the oarsmen in the first boat got the measles. So Frank was promoted to the first boat and the other guy had to stowaway in the baggage car. So they went across country, and they won the nationals.

JY: Then Frank later graduated and was commissioned as a naval officer. I think you said he served in the Pacific?

SUSAN: It was, I believe, after the war was over. He was on the USS McKean, which was a minesweeper. They did not see action, but they were clearing mines in the Pacific.

JY: After his discharge, he went to San Diego?

SUSAN: No. San Francisco. And he got a job with Traveler's Insurance Company.

JY: He was a single man in San Francisco?

SUSAN: Yes. He went to parties here at Board's Crossing with his cousin Nicol Smith.

JY: So Frank and Nicol Smith got to be good friends?

TODD: Yeah. There was a motivation for that. Around that time, R.H. didn't have any money so he took on an investor.

JY: Who is R.H.?

SUSAN: Robert Hays Smith, Nicol Smith's father.

TODD: There was a reason my dad was close to Nicol. Like you said, it would keep him in the social circles.

JY: You two met Nicol Smith here when you were kids. What was he like?

SUSAN: Short, stocky, happy.

TODD: Great big, round face.

SUSAN: Big round face, round belly, chatty, always.

JY: So Nicol Smith bought this property from Frank D. Nicol?

SUSAN: No. Robert Hays Smith bought it from Frank David Nicol's widow. And leveraged it, because he was always wheeling and dealing. The question was how Nicol Smith and his wife got the lien all clear, that R.H. had left on the property.

JY: Nicol Smith's wife was a Standard Oil heiress?

SUSAN: Yeah.

TODD: The genesis of this place doesn't start with Frank D. Nicol. The genesis starts with James Nicol. He was a fruit grower in Gold Springs, across the river.

JY: So James came here?

TODD: He would fish the river, because at the end of the year one of the big markets was selling fruit in Carson City (Nevada), where there was a silver strike. He would take fruit over there in a wagon.

SUSAN: Over Ebbetts Pass

TODD: So he would come down and fish in the North Fork (of the Stanislaus River). So the family knew the north fork. And Frank D. was up here, staying at Big Trees, and he heard about this place and bought it on the spot.

JY: How many acres?

TODD: A quarter-section

JY: And that cabin up the hill. That was built by Frank D.?

TODD: No, that was the original Board's cabin.

JY: Did Frank D. take it over and live there?

TODD: Yeah, he owned this whole thing. It was 160 acres on this side all the way up to Sourgrass bridge.

SUSAN: And Nicol Smith sold part of it.

TODD: He would sell little pieces of land to keep things going.

JY: So James Nicol was the first to discover this property?

TODD: Yeah. He didn't own anything. At that point, the Boards would have owned it. They were running cattle through the crossing. I can remember as a kid, herds of cattle coming through here.

SUSAN: Yeah, we did have cattle coming down.

JY: What years was that?

TODD: Late sixties. It used to happen quite a bit. That's why that road barrier is pushed over up there, by the bridge. Too many cattle were balking.

JY: Back to Berkeley. How did Frank meet your mother?

SUSAN: Frank was working in San Francisco. Frank transferred to Traveler's Insurance in L.A. or Pasadena. One of the things I have in my scrapbook is a letter from Frank McCaffery to Jean, introducing her to Frank, or vice-versa.

JY: Jean was editor of her newspaper at Berkeley?

SUSAN: *The Daily Californian*, during the summer.

JY: She was also student body president?

TODD: While the guys were gone.

JY: She never knew Frank while they were at Cal?

SUSAN: Correct. They had some friends in common. They were there at the same time.

JY: All three of you were born in San Diego?

TODD: Yeah.

SUSAN: La Jolla.

JY: Did he continue to work for Traveler's Insurance?

SUSAN: At some point, he went into partnership with someone and began their own independent insurance agency, Hornaday Nicol Insurance, with Quinn Hornaday.

JY: He later was appointed as Deputy Director for the State Parks?

SUSAN: Deputy Director for two years. Then Director of Veterans Affairs for another six.

JY: Going to Sacramento, was that a big shock for you kids, leaving your friends behind?

SUSAN: Initially, I thought my life was over, because all my friends were in San Diego. The first year was pretty hard for me. But then I started to make friends, and I started to get into school activities. Music and theater.

JY: Todd, was that the time that you and Alan started spending more time here, at Board's Crossing?

TODD: Yeah. I don't remember coming here from San Diego, but Nicol was always part of our vocabulary. Moving to Sacramento was an eye-opening experience, because they were such formative years, for me when I was 9 to 16. So much happened during those years.

JY: Your mom worked for the Voice of America in New York, after graduating from Cal?

SUSAN: Yes, I'm going to say on the Far East desk.

JY: Jean grew up in southern California?

SUSAN: She grew up in Long Beach. I think she went to Long Beach Polytech High School. I have her letters of acceptance from both Berkeley and Stanford. And then, her parents moved to Garden Grove.

JY: What was her dad's name?

SUSAN: Raymond D. Elliott. He was called Pat.

TODD: We called him Pop.

JY: What did Raymond do?

SUSAN: He was a chemist, or chemical engineer. I'm not sure which it was.

TODD: Out of the University of Chicago.

SUSAN: Where he played football. I don't know exactly what got him to California. But he invented a device that would detect when water would come into the well..

TODD: I think it was electronic, and it would send signals when they would hit water.

JY: So it was a money-making device.?

SUSAN: Yeah. So a corporation was formed, called Oilfields Service Company. There were some other partners. At some point one of the big oil service companies was sued by Pop for patent infringement and it was settled. Nobody won. And Pop got I don't know how much money. Enough to get him started in Orange County real estate.

JY: Did he do well in real estate?

TODD: It was wide open. We grew up going to a shopping center. Garden Square. Sooner or later we found out it belonged to our family. There were offices, stores, restaurants, a grocery store, things like that.

JY: Raymond played football at the University of Chicago? Was he a big man?

TODD: He was barrel chested.

JY: When you took your parents ashes and cast them into the Stanislaus River: What was that like for the three of you?

SUSAN: It was poignant. There was some debate as to whether mom wanted to be up here. Because toward the end of her life, with Alzheimer's, she really didn't like it up here. It was always a lot of work. But I think she enjoyed it before she started deteriorating.

JY: What year was she starting to show the Alzheimer's symptoms?

SUSAN: The early 2000's.

JY: At some point, she lost her memory of who Frank was?

SUSAN: Yeah.

JY: What was it like for Frank, taking care of her, all those years?

TODD: It was horrible, because as the disease progressed she started getting paranoid. She thought my dad was somebody else who was a threat.

SUSAN: It was very hard on him. He was unfailing in his desire to take care of her and keep her safe.

TODD: She didn't have the capacity to be close to him. I never remember them holding hands, or hugging.

SUSAN: They weren't especially physically demonstrative.

JY: Todd, you had heard that Teddy Roosevelt was here signing a document at the cabin?

TODD: Yeah, in the old Board's cabin. They all signed their names to one of the planks there, but they took it off because they didn't want it to get stolen.

JY: For Yosemite Park?

TODD: Yeah.

JY: Susan, your dad told you a lot of stories about how rough it was on the ranch, growing up?

SUSAN: Yeah, it was hard work, and it was during the Great Depression. One story he told me, I believe it was in 1929, when aviation had just started. So they were putting a beacon on top of Mount Diablo, because, otherwise, aircraft were going to fly into the mountain. So there was this big buildup to when the beacon was first going to be lit. Dad told the story of how the three kids were out there waiting and waiting for it to go on.

And there's the story of driving to Freestone in one of the old trucks, and they had to back up one of the roads because, whatever kind of car it was, this was probably in the twenties, the way the fuel line went, if you were going uphill at a certain angle, the fuel couldn't get to the engine, so they had to back up.

TODD: And back in the old days in Freestone, great-grandma had a car accident, fell out and busted her leg. Never could walk again on her own. (Carrie Hund)

JY: Todd, you and Alan spent a lot of time here at Board's Crossing, as kids?

TODD: Yeah.

JY: Was Bill Green one of the people you knew? The driver for Nicol Smith?

TODD: Yeah. Valet driver, all-around drunk. But back to the ranch for just a second. Couple of the stories my dad told me. I remember a story they were growing cantaloupe one year.

They would get a car. They would load the car themselves, with ice. There were no refrigerated cars at that time. So you would hook the car up, and it would head back east. And all along the way, they would have to re-ice.

SUSAN: Are you talking about a railroad car?

TODD: Yeah. It was the farmer's liability, until it got to the market. I think it went all across the country. If a car got pulled off to the side, on a spur, the cantaloupe would just die.

JY: But their main crop was almonds?

TODD: Yeah. And walnuts. Another story I remember because it was so poignant. The trees started dying. It became pretty obvious after a while that the water table had risen so far. At that point it was called the Sacramento River, that it killed the roots of the trees. And nothing was irrigated. It was all dryland farming. Obviously not the cantaloupe. I don't know how they did the furrows.

SUSAN: So the tree root system was good enough to get to the water table?

TODD: Yeah.

JY: Did anyone ever talk to you about James George Nicol?

SUSAN: Not until mom started doing her genealogy research.

JY: About Eliza Dodge. She came across the Isthmus of Panama on a mule or horse?

SUSAN: A mule is what I heard.

JY: With a chaperone?

TODD: I've heard that story, too.

SUSAN: When World War II began, Frank was a sophomore at Berkeley. Walter (his brother) was two years younger. So, Walter Nicol's children wonder, how come Frank didn't have to go? Walter either joined or was drafted fairly early.

JY: What unit was Walter in?

TODD: Tank Corps.

SUSAN: So I guess it had to with draft deferrals, if you were in college. And the other side of family wonder why Nicol Smith left this property to just Frank, when he had other cousins? I think it was the friendship that Frank and Nicol had. Frank was a bachelor. Nicol was essentially a bachelor. And Walter had married, while he was serving. And so his life was different. He wasn't going to San Francisco to parties, like Frank was.

TODD: So later on, when Freestone was sold. It happened very quickly, without any talk. And I think that was dad's way of making things right. You take Freestone, I'll take the River and $200,000. That's how he got the money to buy the grove. Dad was always about making peace.

Interview with Garry Nicol

John Young interviewed Garry Nicol at Freestone, CA, on 18 June 2021. Garry's father, Walter, was the son of Lawrence and Irene Nicol.

Following is a transcript of the interview:

JY: I believe you were born on April 22, 1948. Was that Alameda? Or San Francisco?

GARRY: Oakland.

JY: Your full first name is Garrett. I believe that was your mother Elaine's maiden name?

GARRY: Yes. That was my mother's maiden name.

JY: I found a few U.S. census records on your mom, Elaine. She was born in Indiana and was still living there in 1940. When did she move to California?

GARRY: Just at the end of the war. 1945.

JY: Did she marry your dad after she came here?

GARRY: Yes.

JY: When did Walter meet your mom?

GARRY: He was doing some training at Indiana University.

JY: That was an Army Special Training Program?

GARRY: Something like that. I thought it was an officer training program. And then the Army said, forget this, we need bodies in tanks, and sent them to Kentucky, where they did some really quick training, which they felt was inadequate. They put them with tanks on ships and off they went to Europe.

JY: What year was that?

GARRY: That would have been 1944. I think he sent Christmas letters in 1944.

JY: I saw a copy of your dad's WWII draft registration card. He was 18 when he registered in June 1942. Living at 2336 Piedmont Ave in Berkeley, with his parents, Lawrence and Irene Nicol?

GARRY: Yes. He did a year or two of college before he was drafted or enlisted. I think he must have enlisted to get into that special program.

JY: Your dad was in an armored unit?

GARRY: Right.

JY: What did your dad do in the war, and where did he serve? What unit?

GARRY: He said his main job was, he had asbestos gloves, and he would take these hot shells out of the gun. He said he had some kind of machine gun, where he could shoot from inside to outside.

JY: Was he in combat?

GARRY: Yes. I can't say it was a real battle. It was toward the end of the war, and there was a lot of mopping up of nests. The big thing was, he helped liberate Dachau. When we were growing up, there were photos of bodies at Dachau. Boxcars of bodies.

JY: Photos that he took?

GARRY: He said his sergeant took them. All of us kids looked at them, and then eventually, he took them away and burned them.

JY: Did he say much about Dachau?

GARRY: We would ask him about it, and he said there were some Brits there, and the Brits were happy to see them. He didn't say much about it.

JY: Do you recall anything else he said about the war?

GARRY: He said when they were on trains, going from one place to another, there would be French who would trade wine for cigarettes, and it was watered down wine. He said they met up with the Russians and had a big party. He would describe the Americans dancing with great big Russian women soldiers. And I think he did, too.

JY: I saw an article in the *Oakland Tribune*, Sept 1945, which said Walter had just returned from Germany, where he served in the 20th Armored Division.

GARRY: That's right.

JY: Did he attend college at Berkeley after he got home?

GARRY: Yeah. He came back home, and nobody came to meet him at the train station, because his father had put his car up on blocks because of the gas rationing, so he had to walk from the train station out to the family house in Berkeley. He walked across town with his duffel bag.

JY: Were they surprised to see him?

GARRY: Yeah. I think maybe they knew, but not exactly when.

JY: Did he return to college at Berkeley?

GARRY: Yes. He came back in May of 1945. I guess he got leave to come home. He was still in the service when the atom bomb was dropped.

JY: What did he major in?

GARRY: I think he might have been pre-med before the war. He switched to zoology, and he ended up in entomology. He got a B.A. in entomology.

JY: What did Walter do for a living, with his degree?

GARRY: He worked for the mosquito abatement district, in Visalia. He would go around and check people's cesspools and see if there were mosquitos growing. He had a little jeep with no doors, that was fun for me. And then he went to work for Ortho, where he would check farmer's fields and advise them about what insecticides and fertilizers to use. Ortho was part of Standard Oil. Every hardware store usually had a garden department with Ortho stuff. This was more for farmers than homeowners. And that was pretty much his career path. He was in the Silicon Valley area, where there were a lot of orchards, then he was transferred to Casa Grande, Arizona.

The family spent four or five years there. It was just too hot, and he suffered from being out in the heat, so he transferred to Watsonville. That's where he worked mostly with apple orchards.

JY: Watsonville is in northern California?

GARRY: Yes. Santa Cruz County. At some point he tried to go into business for himself. Next door to where we were renting a house was a gas station. I don't know if he bought it or leased it, but he used it as a place for his storage tanks and some insecticides. And he actually ran the gas station, too. He had someone else running the gas station while he was out. And then an Agri farm company pulled out the rug from under him, and he had to give up on that. He knew someone from the education department in the county, and that fellow encouraged him to go back and get a teaching credential, and he did. So he finished his career teaching. He taught the handicapped. There was a farm school at Cabrillo, and he figured he could work there.

JY: These kids were what age range?

GARRY: They had to be 21 to go to Cabrillo. Young adults.

JY: Did Walter talk about what it was like growing up on the almond ranch, in Brentwood?

GARRY: Yeah. The stories never quite matched with Frank's. Frank had to do more work, but my father never had to do much work. I know he got sick at least one summer. They said he had brain fever, and he spent the summer here with Grandpa Frederick, who was a doctor. Maybe because he was the younger one, Frank had to do more work.

JY: Did Walter like it out there, on the almond ranch?

GARRY: Yeah, I think he did.

JY: How old was Walter when they moved to the house on Piedmont?

GARRY: It was after high school. I think he lived at the fraternity. He used the home on Piedmont as their base, during summer, and before going into the service,

JY: What do you recall about your grandparents, Lawrence and Irene?

GARRY: They made a huge impression on all of us. They were fabulously entertaining. Growing up, it was about as much fun as you could have, hanging out with them. Grandpa was a little gruff, but fascinating. Grandpa would rant and rave more. About politics. Maybe family members. I remember going into his bedroom here and seeing his false teeth up on the table. And he would wear a nightgown. In his dresser, he had a pistol from World War I in there. Roman coins, and some gold pieces. He would put sugar on his tomatoes and salt on his watermelon.

JY: Sue and Todd said that Lawrence met her brother, Wallie in France during WWI. They had heard that Wallie Hund was an interrogator and managed to persuade his commander to allow Lawrence to join his unit as an interrogator. Irene Hund Nicol told Jean Nicol that they were both in the "statistical division" in the army. Later, Wallie was transferred to the chemical warfare division because of his chemistry background. What have you heard about how they met, and what they did in France?

GARRY: I don't know. All I remember is that he went to school in the Sorbonne.

JY: But he did meet Wallie in France?

GARRY: They met somewhere over there.

JY: Did you hear if they met in headquarters, or on the battlefield?

GARRY: I don't know.

JY: Lawrence apparently stayed in France after the war ended and studied at the Sorbonne. Do you know what he studied there?

GARRY: No.

Q; How did Irene feel about leaving San Francisco and moving to the almond ranch?

GARRY: I never heard that many complaints about the ranch. They sold it for a good price and moved to the house on Piedmont. They stayed there until the early sixties.

JY: Do you think your grandfather was changed by the war? Is that why he left the city for the almond ranch?

GARRY: I don't think so. No one ever talked about that.

JY: Do you recall Irene playing the piano and singing at parties?

GARRY: Yeah. That was always a big thing. It was great when she had the piano. Then she had the banjo. She played the ukulele, too. Then she got an electric piano, and played it on her lap.

JY: Did Irene like it here at Freestone?

GARRY: Grandma didn't much like it here, because of the limited social life. They lived at the house on Piedmont in Berkeley most of the year.

JY: What is the origin of the "Ossie-Boosie" song that you Nicols sing at family gatherings?

GARRY: That was baby talk from a young cousin. And that turned into Ossie-Boosie. Of course, it's the theme to "Howdy-Doody Time."

JY: Did Irene talk to you about growing up in San Rafael, and their house on Laurel Grove Avenue?

GARRY: She would talk about the earthquake, when she was in bed with her cousin, in Ross. I forget if her father still had a practice in San Francisco or if he was in Ross. He lost a lot of property in San Francisco, but I don't know if he lost his medical office.

JY: Irene told Jean that her parents, Frederick Hund and Carrie Zech Hund, bought the Freestone property about 1910 or 1911. Does that sound right?

GARRY: We understood 1912.

JY: According to what Irene told Jean, Frederick's sons, Wally and Fred, were looking at Freestone as a place where they could grow drugs such as digitalis, mint and belladonna. They planned to manufacture the drugs, but found they couldn't produce enough to make it pay. Did you hear about this story?

GARRY: That sounds right.

JY: How old were you when you began to visit Freestone?

GARRY: I probably came here before I could remember. We came here when I was in Visalia, probably three or four years old. When we lived in Casa Grande, Grandma would send us German cookies and greens from the trees.

JY: Susan mentioned a game you kids played at Freestone, using a toy from Chinatown. You poked it and a piece of paper came out with a task. If you did it, you got to pick an item from the no-touch box, which had things left behind by the girls at the Piedmont boarding house. Do you remember that?

GARRY: Oh, yeah. You had to stand on one foot and tap your stomach and your head at the same time. Funny things like that. Whistle a tune.

JY: So you kids had a good time here at Freestone?

GARRY: Yeah. But the dark side of paradise was the poison oak.

JY: Your dad had a sister, Jean Nicol. What do you recall about her?

GARRY: Auntie Jean was a real character. She loved to smoke and drink and tell stories. So at Ossie-Boosie time, she'd be right in there. A funny sense of humor.

JY: Jean went to the University of California at Berkeley?

GARRY: Yes. I think she was a very active tennis player.

JY: Did she get married before she graduated?

GARRY: I think she got married before she graduated. I'm not sure if she graduated. Everyone was getting married that same summer. My mother wore the same wedding dress that Jean wore. Jean married Pat, and Pat had been in the merchant marines. I think it was Pat that had terrible experiences, seagoing.

JY: Do you know where they lived? Alameda?

GARRY: They lived in Fremont.

JY: Patrick died in 1968?

GARRY: He committed suicide. He had back problems, and I think mental problems, too. They had two daughters, Kathy and Carolyn. In 1971, she married William Saylor.

JY: Did your dad or your grandfather, Lawrence, ever talk about Lawrence's father, Frank David Nicol? What do you recall hearing about him?

GARRY: Not much. Maybe I was too young for some of the stories.

JY: How about James George Nicol, your 2nd great-grandfather, from Scotland? What do you know about him?

GARRY: Nothing, really.

JY: You have a very interesting 2nd great-grandmother, Eliza Lawrence Rogers, who apparently traveled across the Isthmus of Panama on a mule when she was 18, on a journey from Vermont to California. What do you know about her?

GARRY: We had heard that story. She was a teacher in Columbia, And we heard that when she rode her mule to the school to teach, the miners would come out and tip their hats. She was about the only woman around. A big deal.

Interview with Susan Nicol

John Young interviewed Susan Nicol Thibodeaux on 10 March 2022, Tucson, AZ

Following is a transcript of the interview:

JY: Can you describe your home in San Diego?

SUSAN: I guess it was a typical California home. We had a little backyard with a swing set. That's where the barbecue was. Sometimes in warm weather, we would play in the sprinklers. The house had three bedrooms. My brothers shared a bedroom. There was a living room/dining room, with a fireplace.

JY: How far from the beach were you?

SUSAN: To get to the beach or get to the surf, you go to Mission Beach or Ocean Beach.

JY How far from your school?

SUSAN: We would walk to school, Sunset View Elementary, which I think was less than a mile.

JY: What sort of things did you do as a family?

SUSAN: I don't remember doing a lot. When we took vacations, when we lived in San Diego, we would usually go up to northern California to visit Grandma and Grandpa Nicol. And, we would see the family at Freestone. There was always the Halloween festival at school. The Halloween carnival. At which the PTA raised money. Mom was president of the PTA at Sunset View. We hardly ever went out to dinner. We only went to Naty's Mexican food, which was down closer to the beach.

JY: Was that by choice, or for financial reasons?

SUSAN: I think it was partly financial reasons. In those days, people didn't go out to dinner much. Mom was home. She had volunteer activities with the PTA and the Junior League. She was very active in that.

JY: What was the Junior League?

SUSAN: Junior League is a service organization that exists throughout the country. You age out of it at age 40. It's about helping young women serve the community. It gives them the opportunity to develop their skills, supporting the community.

JY: What do you remember about your mom growing up in San Diego?

SUSAN: She was engaged in a lot of things. She was busy. She was supportive of my brother's playing baseball. When I was doing chorus at school, she was always helping, and helping us with our homework. She helped me when I needed it. When I was having trouble with my multiplication tables, she helped me study, and I got them all quickly memorized after that.

JY: I believe you once told me she was very strict on grammar?

SUSAN: Yeah, she was. I think I remember that more when we were older. Even into adulthood, she would correct us. In terms of usage, me versus I, lay versus lie, all that kind of stuff.

JY: So, you're pretty much the way she was?

SUSAN: Yeah. That's why I correct you.

JY: Back to when you first moved to Sacramento, do you recall that?

SUSAN: Yeah. That was back in 1968, when Reagan got elected as governor. Dad went up and started working, and we stayed to finish out the school year. That was my sixth grade. Todd and Alan were fourth and second. We moved up there in June.

JY: How did you feel about moving?

SUSAN: I don't remember thinking it was going to be a problem when we moved up, but when I got up there, I felt it was a problem. I felt like I didn't have friends. I wasn't good at making friends, and I never had to make friends before. I had been through school with all the same people. It took a year to feel more comfortable with that. After four years, when Reagan got elected again, that subject came up at the dinner table one night, Like how do you all feel about moving back to San Diego after the first four years? And I was so upset, I jumped up and left the dinner table. I was so upset because I had made friends, I was in choir and school. I was going to audition for the Madrigals. I think I had been in a musical already. So I thought it was going to be the worst unfairness in the world. I was quite dramatic about it.

JY: What happened after that?

SUSAN: Well, we didn't move.

JY: Because of you?

SUSAN: I don't know. I wasn't involved in the decision process.

JY: How did your mom feel about moving from San Diego to Sacramento?

SUSAN: My impression was that she initially thought it was exciting. But eventually, she was not all that impressed with many of the political people. There were some who were good friends and stayed good friends for a long time. But many of them, not so much.

JY: She worked at the Voice of America after college, and then worked at the alumni office in Pasadena. So she was a professional until she got married, then she was a housewife. Did she regret not working again in a professional career?

SUSAN: I think absolutely she regretted it. I think Dad did not want her to work. He didn't think that was appropriate or necessary. It was the fifties. I think she felt cheated. The late sixties were the beginning of "women's liberation." I think she thinks she missed out. I think her self-fulfillment ultimately came from doing the research involved in choosing the property in Pauma Valley. To buy and build the house on it. She pretty much acted as the general contractor for building the house. She worked with an architect. It was an artistic and financial project that was her baby. And subsequently, when they bought the surrounding property, she imagined and put into motion the growing and developing of the avocado grove.

JY: So when they moved to Pauma Valley, first they bought the house and later bought the land for the avocado grove?

SUSAN: Right.

JY: How much later was that?

SUSAN: Ten years.

JY: Was it her decision to grow the avocados?

SUSAN: I think they were looking for a source of income and Mom did a lot of research on the water availability in Pauma Valley and the avocado market. I think she felt strongly that they needed more income, and she thought it was a good investment. Her trust money had been managed by her brother, and he was very speculative on a lot of things, and lost a lot of her money.

JY: That was John Elliott?

SUSAN: Yeah. So she wanted to do her own thing.

JY: Was that trust money from Raymond Elliott? Did she get enough money from that to buy the property at Pauma Valley?

SUSAN: No. So, her money was used to buy the property and build the house. The avocado property came to be the result of Irene (Hund Nicol) dying. So that property (in Freestone) was left to Frank, Walter and Jean. So it made no sense for all those three children to own Freestone. So they did property trades, which is a good tax advantage. So, Walter essentially bought out Jean Saylor and Frank Nicol. So it was Dad's money that bought the property (for the avocado grove). And additional money was needed to plant, to do the irrigation, to pay for all that until the trees started producing. And that additional investment came from Mom's family, from Oilfields Service.

JY: When your parents lived in Pauma Valley, they joined the country club?

SUSAN: Yeah. Perhaps not immediately, but they did. They figured out that was the way to get to know people.

JY: So they had a lot of friends there?

SUSAN: They did. And Pauma Valley grew a lot during the thirty years that they lived there. It was not as fancy-schmancy a club or residential area when they first moved there.

JY: I know they were good friends with Tom and Nancy Ellington. And Nancy helped your mother after she had Alzheimer's?

SUSAN: Mom and Dad met the Ellingtons when they built their house about ten years after my parents did. So that was about the time they had the avocado property, and the Ellingtons were walking their dog on Nicol property, and that's how they met. They were trespassing. So they became friends. Went to events at the country club together, had dinner at each other's houses. At that point, they were early seventies, so they were able to be more social and participate in things. In the subsequent twenty years, they were older, and younger people started joining the country club and moving into the area. So that wasn't quite as good a match, socially.

JY: But your parents were sociable people. Especially Frank, as I recall. He always had a happy hour, as I recall.

SUSAN: Yeah, he had a happy hour. He loved to have parties, and go to parties. And that was a burden on Mom. I think she felt that was just a lot of work for her. That's how she felt about going to Board's Crossing and having company there. How much of that was the beginning of Alzheimer's, it's hard to know.

JY: When did you first realize she had Alzheimer's?

SUSAN: Todd and Frank started to see it in the early 2000s. She would forget things. Put Tupperware in the oven. And not take care of things she used to take care of. They both noticed that and stepped up to do more. Prior to that, she had been doing the books, paying bills, as well as taking care of the household. Taking care of the financial things started falling apart. Her ability to understand who was who started falling apart. So for a number of years I came over to help get the tax stuff together. Which was good for me to be in touch with what was going on in the business.

JY: You were living in Tucson then?

SUSAN: Yeah. I would come over for at least one long weekend. And one year I came over and had to recreate all the records from August on. It was toast. So after that we hired Todd's girlfriend Helen to pay the bills and do the QuickBooks. I still came over to do the taxes and get things ready for the accountant. By 2006, she was certainly compromised cognitively. I remember in 2007 or 2008 I flew over on a Friday night. She waited up for me, and we talked in the living room. We chatted for a while. And it became clear she really didn't know who I was. She said, so, where are you living these days? I said I'm still in Tucson. Still working at Raytheon. She said, Oh. My daughter lives in Tucson. Of course that was upsetting, but I pivoted and said, yeah, I know her. She's doing really great. She's a great person. I think she said, you know, she divorced her husband. I said, yeah, I did hear that.

JY: Your mom came to visit you at your home in 2009?

SUSAN: Yes. She came over by herself, which was probably a little risky. I hired a woman to stay with her during the day when I went to work. We had a good time. We bought some things for the house. Gave Dad a break.

JY: What do you think prompted her genealogy research?

SUSAN: I don't know. I think it was in 1996, she and I went to Scotland, and she followed up on that research. But she probably started genealogy research prior to that. Because, when we went to Europe in the summer of 1976, we went to Germany, and to Homberg. So she had started it much earlier. After they moved back to San Diego in 1975. I think she should have gone to law school and learned about water rights, because she was very interested in that. But the years that are most vivid to me are the years she was deteriorating. It was hard for her. She really didn't know who Dad was. She thought he was a cousin. She was worried he was going to take her house.

JY: So she didn't know who your Dad was during her last several years?

SUSAN: Correct. And uncomfortable before that. I really couldn't tell you when that started. They shared the same bedroom until she started falling. She slept on the couch after that. She fell a couple of times, then went into a nursing home, then came back to the house. Which, in hindsight, if they had sold in 2007, they could have sold that house and property for a lot more than we ended up selling it. Real estate hadn't crashed, the water crunch hadn't started, and they could have been in a safer place for them. But they didn't want to leave, and Mom thought, if anyone takes away my house, it's not okay.

JY: So they had floated the idea to her?

SUSAN: Yeah. But Mom really didn't want to leave. It was her baby. And Dad wanted Mom to be happy. He did whatever he could to keep her happy. With all her credentials, she lived in an era where women just didn't go for it. To some extent, Dad discouraged that. That's what the fifties were like. Then she was busy supporting a political life. And she was busy with three kids. She did everything she could to help her children get to a place in life where they could be happy.

Interview: Lawrence Nicol

In May 1974, Susan Nicol, Lawrence Nicol's grand-daughter, interviewed Lawrence at his home in Walnut Creek, California. Also present were Irene Nicol, his wife, Frank Nicol, his son, and Jean Elliott Nicol, Susan's mother. Frank and Jean contributed to the interview.

On the cassette tape, Susan said she was writing a paper on the history of her family for a class at Stanford, where she was a freshman.

Following is a transcript of the interview:

SUSAN: What do you remember about your grandfather, James Nicol?

LAWRENCE: He had a sandy red beard. He was a miner. Then he got some horses and big wagons and took fruit that he grew, apples and pears, and went over the summit to the Comstock, where he sold them. He got about a dollar apiece for each apple. I was a very small boy when I last saw him. And I remember seeing these wagons with great big high wheels.

JEAN: What about your grandmother, Margaret?

LAWRENCE: She died when I was very young. I don't remember her at all.

FRANK: What do you remember about Eliza Rogers Dodge?

LAWRENCE: She left home in Vermont, and crossed the Isthmus of Panama. When she reached Panama on the east coast, they had to take this trail. There was yellow fever rampant at that time. She told me that half of them died on the trail before they got to the Pacific side. They came up the coast to San Francisco. Then she went up into the mines. I don't know what prompted her to go up there. She married this doctor, a Harvard graduate (Mark Tyler Dodge). Shortly after their marriage, mother was born (Adelaide Dodge). And my uncle Henry (Washington H. Dodge), in Jamestown; they called it "Jimtown" at that time.

My grandmother was one of a very small handful of women in that area. There were thousands of miners, but very few women. And he was the only doctor at that time. He had to do all kinds of work on patients under primitive conditions. He had to operate on the kitchen table. She helped him with his instruments and all that. She became very knowledgeable in that field. Suddenly he died, and she was alone.

She told me about one night some Mexicans came to the door around midnight. They said they had an injured comrade. She opened the door and two Mexicans came in, carrying another one. His leg was dangling. Crushed. She told them the doctor was dead, and to take him to the kitchen table. She cut his leg off, sewed him up and saved his life.

She had an infallible nature and was absolutely fearless. I can verify that by an experience I had in Stockton. When I was a small child we lived on the outskirts of Stockton, and a great many tramps used to come down from Sacramento. Most of them were harmless, but there was some bad ones among them. Our house was burglarized three times. One night she heard a noise about midnight in the kitchen. Instead of rousing father, she took a pistol and slipped down to the back stairway. She opened the door to the kitchen and this fellow flew out, and she took a shot at him. The next morning we found that he had carved a hole through the back door so he could get his hand in there. She didn't say much about it. I guess women had to be that way at that time or they wouldn't survive. She was a pretty woman, but she had a mind more like a man.

FRANK: She become a school teacher?

LAWRENCE: Yes, after he died.

SUSAN: What about your father, when you were growing up?

LAWRENCE: I know he began his law practice in Sonora, and he walked four miles every day from Columbia to Sonora to get his education in law. I think he was the youngest lawyer ever accepted into the State Legislature. He married my mother and moved down to Stockton.

SUSAN: What about when you were growing up? You had brothers and sisters?

LAWRENCE: Yes. They're all gone now.

SUSAN: What kind of house did you live in in Stockton?

LAWRENCE: We moved into a house at 1045 Madison Street, where the family lived until he died.

SUSAN: When you were growing up, where did you visit, on holidays?

LAWRENCE: Sometimes we would go to Sonora. Sometimes we would go to San Francisco. Until we got the automobile, there wasn't much traveling around. The first automobiles came out in 1906.

SUSAN: What about school?

LAWRENCE: When I went in the first grade, it was a little wooden school, with only two classrooms. That was about 1896. They had a pump outside, where you got your drinking water.

SUSAN: Was it always planned for you to go to college?

LAWRENCE: My father was a lawyer, but I wasn't too anxious to study law. My father wanted me to. Then I went into the first world war.

FRANK: When you were in high school, and there was no transportation, what did you do in the evening?

LAWRENCE: We had social gatherings once in a while. If you wanted to go hunting, you could go to the livery stable and get a horse and start out. We had these high school parties. Social functions at the schools. Then the neighbors would get together. It was a more neighborly atmosphere then. The home was the central gathering place. The family didn't need so much. There was a closer tie-in to the family units at that time. I thought it was a good thing.

SUSAN: Was there anyone living with your family besides your mother and father and your broth and sisters?

LAWRENCE: Eliza's husband died early and left her with those two small children, and she had to raise them under difficult conditions in Sonora. So later my grandmother moved down to Stockton, after my parents were married. She came down with them. And lived with us until she died.

SUSAN: What kinds of things did she do in the house? Did she help take care of the children and cook?

LAWRENCE: Yes, she did. Mother was more or less a semi-invalid as far back as I can remember. In many ways, my grandmother was more of a mother to me than my own mother was. Grandmother had many outside activities. She was a brilliant woman. She was president of the women's club, and the Philatelist club. She was a very informed woman.

JEAN: I've heard that your mother had a great deal of difficulty delivering her children.

LAWRENCE: I think she was a victim of the ignorance of all those country doctors.   Before she died, when it was too late to do anything for her, we had three of the leading doctors from San Francisco out to diagnose the case. They had a conference there, and I can remember, they said what the doctors had told her was all nonsense.   She was a victim of these country doctors, who didn't know what they were talking about.   Her medicine cabinet was always crowded with all kinds of pills and medicines.

FRANK: You were telling me you used to go up on the train or the buckboard to stay with relatives in Sonora?

LAWRENCE: I can remember visiting Uncle Ned (Rogers) up there. I remember his office had these two great iron doors. He would lock them with this big key and go around with that big key. All those who knew him recalled that he was a brilliant man. He could recite the Bible from one end to the other, by heart.

I wish I could have recorded the things they said at the dinner table. They were very interesting. Grandmother knew all the old-timers up there. I was too young to realize the historic value of all that.

One thing I recall, Grandmother told me she used to ride horseback to ride down from her home to teach school. There was a big oak tree with a hanging limb. On that trail, she saw some objects hanging down, and she approached and found that the vigilante committee had hung three desperados and they were swinging from that big limb.

What these vigilantes did was for the benefit of the entire community. That reminds me of something happening right now. It was more effective than anything they are doing these days in San Francisco. Hanging would have a quicker effect than anything else..

FRANK: With there being no automobiles, did everybody have a barn with a horse in it?

LAWRENCE: Yeah.

FRANK: How many did you have?

LAWRENCE: Just one horse and a donkey.

FRANK: What did you do with the donkey?

LAWRENCE: It was for the children to ride.

JEAN: Did your father have a fancy little buggy?

LAWRENCE: No. His office was only a few blocks away. And they had the streetcar. It was pulled by horses. They had street sweepers at that time. They did nothing but keep the streets clean. Because cars were scarce, the atmosphere was clear as a bell. No fumes. In 1907 the first automobiles arrived, but they were so scarce, you could hardly see one.

JEAN: How did you get from Stockton to Berkeley? By train?

LAWRENCE. Yeah. The Santa Fe. When I came down on that in 1907, to go to college, there were places that hadn't been built but a few years, and they found some of the tracks had been built over peat moss, which was drained. They had to dump thousands of pounds of gravel to sustain the trains.

SUSAN: Was your father the disciplinarian, or was your grandmother?

LAWRENCE: My grandmother took care of it.

JEAN: It sounds like your father was a very active man.

LAWRENCE. Oh, so active. He had to travel. He had clients in Modesto. He was an outstanding lawyer. Several of the leading lawyers in San Francisco begged him to go down, and go in with them. Because he was a genius. A friend said, you can't work day and night. You've got to get out and get some exercise, and take a vacation. You can't carry this load. He said he didn't have time.

JEAN: Could you tell us about the changes, from that time?

LAWRENCE: We had an old wood-burning stove, to heat the water. In fact, we even had a pump, in one part of the kitchen.

FRANK: The well was underneath the house? It didn't come from the city?

LAWRENCE: Yes. We had no electricity. Finally got a telephone. A great big wooden one on the wall. We had to heat the water for the bath tub on the stove.

JEAN: What about groceries?

LAWRENCE: The milkman came around, took the milk out of a great big can, poured it in big pans, and we would skim the cream off these pans. Then the bread man would come around in a wagon, every day, with four or five shelves in the back.

JEAN: Horse-drawn?

LAWRENCE: Yeah. Then the iceman would come with these huge chunks of ice. He had a scale and a big saw. If you wanted ten pounds, or twenty, he'd saw this up. Then he had ice tongs, to carry the big blocks of ice. Then for the vegetables, the Chinese handled the vegetables. They had wicker baskets, one on each end of this long pole.

JEAN: What did you do for meat? Did they come around door-to-door?

LAWRENCE: Yeah, they did.

SUSAN: Do you remember the first radios?

LAWRENCE: In the mid-twenties, when radios first became available, they were pretty complicated. Lots of dials. There were only one or two stations anyway. Up until that time, in the evening, usually people would take turns reading out loud. They would be entertained by listening.

SUSAN: What do you remember about the first cars?

LAWRENCE: I remember a lot of Model Ts, and Maxwells. A lot of horses.

SUSAN: What was the Berkeley campus like when you attended Cal?

LAWRENCE: It was a very small campus. The library, and the science building, that's all that was there. I lived in a home with some friends from Stockton, on Bancroft, right across from the university.

JEAN: What did you do, socially? Did you play football?

LAWRENCE: They switched to rugby, right after I went in. They played rugby most of the time.

SUSAN: After you graduated, did you practice law for a while?

LAWRENCE: Just a short time before I went to war.

JEAN: In San Francisco?

LAWRENCE: Yeah.

SUSAN: You were in the Army?

LAWRENCE: Yeah. For sixteen months.

JEAN: And you met grandma's brother while you were there?

LAWRENCE: In a little French town. A soldier said, there's a fellow from California I want you to meet. It was dark out there. So that's how we met. We got to be pretty good friends before we were through. He made me promise when I got back to come to Ross and meet the family. He came home before I did. I stayed and went to Sorbonne. When I got back, I rang him up, and that's when I met her (Irene).

JEAN: At the time of World War I, a lot of changes were taking place in the United States. The industrial revolution was well underway. Cars, radio. How did this affect you and your family? When did you get your first car?

LAWRENCE: In 1920.

JEAN: You met momma. Got married. Why did you move to Brentwood?

LAWRENCE: I was going to stay out there for a year or two and get rich on the almond ranch. I fellow I knew in college was a farm advisor from Contra Costa County. He told me about a wonderful place out there that was a wonderful bargain. He took me out there and got me into it.

SUSAN: When you came back, had you already decided that you didn't want to practice law?

LAWRENCE: Yes. I didn't want to go into an office anymore. I never should have. I'm an outdoor man.

FRANK: What kind of car did you get in 1920?

LAWRENCE: A Model-T. I'll tell you it was a hard life out there. In 1920, the farmers were the first people to suffer from the effects of the Depression. Long before it hit the businesses in the city. From 1920 until 1929, agriculture was just going from bad to worse. The worst eight or ten years I ever went through.

In spite of all that, you got plenty of outdoor exercise and it kept you in good physical shape. You have some intangible gains you don't realize when you're going through those hard times.

Irene's father, (Dr. Frederick Hund), he was a retired a doctor, and he told me, when I was complaining about the heat and the hard work, and the summer was terrifically hot, and I was perspiring, he said, you don't realize, but that's going to extend your life. He says, you'll live ten years longer on account of that. It turned out just that way. My sisters and my brother was sedentary. They didn't like to exercise. I think that's why they all died sooner than I did. I'll be 86 before long. The old man was right. It's how you live those early years that sustains you through the later years.

JEAN: How did the Depression affect your family? We know it affected agriculture, but conversely, you had enough to eat?

LAWRENCE: We didn't grow enough of the things we needed. We went into an irrigated district. We were growing food, but we were not growing vegetables. In the old days, you would grow everything to sustain yourself. You had sheep for wool, you had your chickens, you had your cows. You had your corn. You could sustain yourself. But they created these irrigation districts, and the farmers went into specialty crops. They would have all apricots, or all peaches, or all almonds.

When the Depression came on, I remember a farmer across the way had a beautiful outdoor peach orchard. After the Depression got so bad he couldn't even hired the labor to pick his peaches, and they all fell on the ground. You would see a great golden circle of peaches under every tree. That was the vulnerability of farming, when farmers turned to specialty crops in this country. It wasn't that way in the old days.

SUSAN: When Daddy was born, and Uncle Walter, too, what sort of things did they do on the ranch? Did they have a lot of chores?

LAWRENCE: Oh yeah. The boys would take care of the water, and the irrigation lines. When the crops were harvested, taking care of the crops, and the animals. They had good times, too.

SUSAN: What was the house on the ranch like?

LAWRENCE: The first wasn't too hot. It was old. Made of wood. It had a long hallway, with rooms and doors on one side, like a miniature hotel. You would come into through the front door to the living room and head straight back to the kitchen. There was a big porch outside, a screened porch. The other house we had later was more modern.

SUSAN: When did you move into the second house?

LAWRENCE: We had to sell half the ranch, during the Depression. We couldn't sell the crops. The farmers were in a terrible condition. That was in 1929, after the crash. Farmers were losing the ranches, foreclosures. Businesses were stagnating. People going broke right and left. We had 600 acres. We lost half of that. We had to leave the house on that half. We had to move to this other house across the way, on the other 300 acres. If the Depression had gone on much longer, we would have lost the rest of it.

SUSAN: When you lived on the ranch, you went to Freestone for Christmas and things?

LAWRENCE: Yeah. That's where we would all meet up for Christmas. Then we had the property down in Berkeley. We were there for thirty years, at the place on Piedmont Avenue. We moved there in 1941.

SUSAN: On the ranch, did you have hired hands?

LAWRENCE: Mostly during the harvest. We harvested almonds. First we had horses. We had a water wagon pulled by the horses, before we had irrigation lines. Then we got tractors and got out of the horse business.

When we went out there, it was the end of the horse era. The first tractors up there had iron wheels. They didn't have any rubber. A year or two after that they came out with rubber tires.

FRANK: The steel wheels were getting stuck all the time?

LAWRENCE: They were terrible. But one tractor replaced a dozen horses.

FRANK: Remember back in the beginning, we had the cows, horses, turkeys and chickens and sheep. I don't think we had any of those after about 1925.

LAWRENCE: We got into the irrigation district, and we had to get rid of the sheep. Then we got rid of the horses.

SUSAN: When you went to Freestone on holidays, who all was there?

LAWRENCE: Irene's folks, who were living there. Irene's brothers would come up there. Uncle Walter and his family. Jean and her friends. We had some Christmas parties up there.

SUSAN: Did you handle the discipline in the family?

LAWRENCE: They were all good children. No trouble. Irene handled them in such a way that when she told them to do something, they did it.

SUSAN: What was the summer like on the ranch?

LAWRENCE: One thing that was so hard, in the heat of the summer, when the flies would fly around the meat wagon. We didn't have refrigeration. That was one of the more unpleasant features of that life. We used to talk about the day that would come when we would have refrigeration.

SUSAN: Grandma, what kinds of things would you do on the ranch?

IRENE: I had babies. (laughs) And no conveniences there. Half the time we didn't have any water. . .if baby-sitters had been in style in those days, we wouldn't have had any money to pay them. . .I used to drive your father to school. Four miles each way.

SUSAN: (talking to Frank) You told me you always walked.

FRANK: Once in a while.

LAWRENCE: We had a mortgage on the ranch. We didn't have any money for Christmas one year. We had to go down to the Bank of America and get a loan.

IRENE: We never had any paper money in the West. It was a rarity to see paper money. Grandpa (Dr. Hund) always had his purse with gold coins.

LAWRENCE: You got paid in gold or silver coins. They never tried to pay you in paper.

JEAN: When did things start to turn for the better at the ranch?

LAWRENCE: In 1934. The Big Depression started in 1929, got worse in 1930, and reached its bottom in 1932. Then Roosevelt closed the banks in March 1933. And then things began to perk up.

JEAN: And then you were able to sell some of your crops?

LAWRENCE. Yeah.

SUSAN: How long after that were you still on the ranch?

LAWRENCE: 1941.

JEAN: I suppose the ranch appreciated in value?

LAWRENCE: I sold, got out in cash. Went down and bought that Piedmont property (in Berkeley).

JEAN: When you went to Berkeley, the children went to school there too?

LAWRENCE: The war came on. Then they all went into the service.

SUSAN: What were you doing in Berkeley?

LAWRENCE: Tried to find a way to buy property down there, to make a living. Had no trouble after that.

IRENE: You bought that apartment house, next to the Grant Hotel.

LAWRENCE: Yeah. I bought that before I bought the other. Yeah, that was a good move. Doubled my money. Everything I bought down there paid out.

SUSAN: How long did you work, Grandma?

IRENE: A couple of years. I guess I worked from 1942 to 1945. And you (Lawrence) were a production engineer.

SUSAN: Where did you work?

LAWRENCE: I was making parts for Liberty ships. Machinist work. Helping the war.

SUSAN: Did you always have tenants living at your house on Piedmont?

IRENE: Oh no. We didn't have anybody living there until 1953. We remodeled the house in 1958.

FRANK: During the war, you had the boys in the basement.

LAWRENCE. Yeah.

SUSAN: Grandma, what did you do during World War II, in Berkeley?

IRENE: I was on the draft board.

LAWRENCE: Susan, You'll soon be going to college as a sophomore?

SUSAN: In September.

LAWRENCE: Time flies. When you look back, time flies before you realize it.

SUSAN: When did you come back from the war, from France?

IRENE: He came back in the fall of 1919. . .and when we went to the almond ranch, I thought, well that's for a year or two and enough of that.

LAWRENCE: Then the Depression came.

FRANK: When you left Berkeley, who bought your property on Piedmont?

LAWRENCE: The university. Real estate prices were sky high.

FRANK: Did you hear how your grandfather, James Nicol, arrived in California?

LAWRENCE: He came across in a covered wagon. My father (Frank D. Nicol) used to tell me about all the sights that he saw, the buffalo and all that, but it was all make believe because he wasn't old enough to remember any of that. He heard his father (James) telling about those experiences. He thought he remembered it. He was there, but he was a small child, and he couldn't remember anything. I never heard much about that.

SUSAN: Do you remember your father's brother, Uncle George?

LAWRENCE: Yes. He married a Jewish lady. There was something wrong with her health. He was a very good judge. He was so popular, he was a judge for more than thirty years. He was a big Scotsman, with a red face He'd swagger up and down the street. I was a small boy, but I recall everyone said, "Good Morning Judge."

JEAN: Do you remember uncle Ned Rogers? Somebody tried to assassinate him?

LAWRENCE: He was walking up the street, in front of the old brick building where his office was. He got about halfway up and someone, a would-be assassin sprang out and shot at him point blank. It struck his watch, which reflected the bullet and knocked him down. Saved his life.

JEAN: He was a lawyer but owned a mine. Apparently there was a dispute going on.

LAWRENCE: He was quite a colorful personality.

Interview: Frank and Jean

Susan Nicol interviewed her parents, Frank and Jean, in their car after interviewing Lawrence and Irene Nicol in May 1974.

Following is a transcript of the interview:

SUSAN: I don't understand. Did Grandpa have a partner in on the ranch?

FRANK: Yeah. Uncle Bob. (Robert Hays Smith, the husband of Lawrence Nicol's sister, Susan Nicol Smith.)

JEAN: A part owner.

SUSAN: Where was he?

JEAN: San Francisco.

FRANK: He was investing in all kinds of projects. My father worked for him for a time. It's very complicated because things were starting to go bad for him, so he didn't keep up the payments he was supposed to be making on the ranch. My father and mother invested all their money in it. They had been pretty careful about saving money. She told me once she had twenty thousand dollars when they got married. Which was quite a bit for those days. They pumped everything into the ranch, and things started to go bad, and on top of that, Uncle

Bob hadn't kept up the payments, of his part. Whatever the arrangement was.

SUSAN: Grandma went to Berkeley?

FRANK: Yeah.

JEAN: This was Robert Hays Smith, Uncle Bob?

FRANK: Yeah. He got over-committed. He couldn't pay anybody anything. He had property everywhere. And he couldn't do anything with property. He couldn't even give it away.

SUSAN: Dad, you went to Berkeley. How often did you go back to the ranch?

FRANK: Other than the holidays, the end of the semester. They would come to Berkeley frequently. They would come down for events. My sister was in school. Finally they moved there.

SUSAN: Did they move because they got tired of the ranch?

FRANK: No, because financial conditions made it necessary to sell. Meanwhile, Uncle Bob had to turn over his interest to some other people.

JEAN: I think they had a majority interest.

FRANK: I think my father just gave over the ranch to them but got eighty acres free and clear. Which he then sold.

SUSAN: What kinds of things did you do while you were at Berkeley?

FRANK: I was very happy there. The boat crew, the letterman society, fraternity house, various campus service organizations.

Very few people had automobiles. There were one or two rich boys whose parents gave them cars for high school graduation, but outside of that, nobody had any. There were quite a few boys and girls who lived in nearby towns: Piedmont, Berkeley, and we would visit them, on weekends. Generally, everybody did everything. If you were going to have a football rally, everybody would go. Ten thousand people would go to the football rallies. The football team would be there. The coaches, the band. A roaring bonfire. The freshmen always wore a beanie (hat). Then when you went to the football game, everybody wore a rooter's hat, which was another kind of beanie.

JEAN: The rooting sections were segregated. The men were in the middle, and girls on both sides. Everybody had on a white shirt or blouse. The girls all had pom-poms. They finally got integrated. During the war, there weren't enough men to fill the rooting section.

SUSAN: What happened when all the men left?

JEAN: Well, it was very different. From a school of eighteen or twenty thousand, it got down to six or seven thousand. There was the ROTC program. So there were quite a few men on campus, but they were in uniform. There was the ASTP (Army Specialized Training Program), and Uncle Walter was in that. Then they sent him to Indiana. That's where he met Elaine. So it was quite different. In the first place, you went to school year around. You had a week off between semesters. If you went out to dinner, you had to be in by seven o'clock, and lights out by ten.

SUSAN: Did you graduate before you went into the Navy?

FRANK: I graduated before I went on active duty, but I signed up shortly after the war started in 1942. I was in a Navy reserve program which allowed you to finish school, or until as such time as they needed you, because they couldn't take in everybody at once. Fifteen million men went in, and you can't take in fifteen million men at the same time.

SUSAN: Did you go into training right after you graduated?

FRANK: Yeah.

SUSAN: How long did you train?

FRANK: For a long time. I was in one Navy school after another for about a year. By the time I got through the officer's school, it was late 1944. Then, destroyers were being built. I was on one of them. I went to three different torpedo schools before I even got on a ship.

JEAN: Gearing up for a war is a tremendous logistical battle. Getting men uniformed, armed and trained. It doesn't always work smoothly.

FRANK: A crew was assigned maybe a year before the ship was finished. And various segments of the crew were in training in different parts of the country. And finally the crew all came together at Treasure Island. And then, eventually, we all got on a train and went to Seattle and took over the ship. At Bremerton.

SUSAN: Seattle? They were built there?

FRANK: No. That just happened to be where that one was built.

SUSAN: How long were you on the ship?

FRANK: U.S.S. McKean. From January of 1945 to 1946. Something like that. About eighteen months, I guess.

SUSAN: And then you were discharged?

FRANK: Yeah. Then I went looking for a job. In San Francisco. That's when I started working for the insurance company. There were lots of jobs available. It was locating something of interest to you. The war had gone on for so long, and the economy had been limited for so long, and there were such a large number of men going back to college, production was increasing everywhere, there was inflation, and there was a shortage of all sorts of things. During the war, automobiles had not been produced, except for the military. All of a sudden, there was a demand for millions of automobiles. You had to go on a long waiting list for an automobile. You would get one maybe a year later.

SUSAN: You worked in San Francisco for three years, for Industrial Indemnity?

FRANK: Yeah, and then I worked for St. Paul Fire and Marine insurance company and eventually got down to San Diego with them.

SUSAN: Why did you switch to St. Paul Fire and Marine?

FRANK: I wasn't particularly happy with what I was doing there. And they weren't very happy with me.

SUSAN: Why?

FRANK: I just didn't like doing what they wanted me to do.

SUSAN: What were you doing?

FRANK: I was representing the company to the various insurance agents and brokers in San Francisco. But I was having to promote insurance I didn't care for. I didn't think it was worth it for anybody to buy.

JEAN: What kind?

FRANK: I think it was when the private insurance companies were writing the state disability insurance. I didn't think they were very good.

SUSAN: When you were in San Francisco, where did you live?

FRANK: I lived in Berkeley with the family for a while, and then moved into a flat in San Francisco with Carter Thatcher and Floyd Seymour. And John Bruner. And then I moved to Los Angeles.

SUSAN: Where did you live?

FRANK: I lived in a little apartment not too far from the office.

SUSAN: Downtown?

FRANK: In the Wilshire District.

SUSAN: Is that where you lived when you met mom?

FRANK: Yes.

JEAN: You used to go on trips.

FRANK: Santa Barbara, and Santa Maria. San Luis Obispo.

About the Author

John T. Young

After graduating high school in Clovis, New Mexico, John Young joined the U.S. Army Security Agency in 1968 and served one tour in Vietnam.

Following his discharge in 1972, he attended the University of Arizona, where he majored in journalism and worked as a reporter for the *Arizona Daily Star*, during and after college.

In the 1980s, he was a writer for the U.S. Information Agency and a reporter for the Voice of America in Washington,

D.C. Later, he became a police officer and private investigator in New Mexico. After the 9/11 attacks, he joined the FBI as a counter-terrorism analyst and worked at the National Counter Terrorism Center.

He subsequently moved over to the Defense Intelligence Agency and was trained in operations as a human intelligence collector. He served two tours in Iraq with the Joint Special Operations Command, working missions targeting Al-Qaida and other terrorist groups.

After Iraq, John was an instructor for U.S. Army Intelligence at Ft. Huachuca, Arizona until he retired. His first novel, *Indian Country*, won an award in the Arizona Literary contest and was subsequently published by Ingram & Elliott. John has published two other novels about terrorism and crime: *The Nexus* and *Princess of Poland*.

Notes

Chapter 1

[1] New Orleans, Passenger Lists, 1813-1963, database, *Ancestry* (http://www.ancestry.com : accessed 23 Mar 2021) entry for James George McNicol, age 19, arrived 20 Dec 1844, New Orleans, Louisiana, aboard the *Oakland.*

[2] California, U.S., Voter Registers, 1866-1898 for James G. Nicol, California State Library; Sacramento, California; *Great Registers, 1866-1898;* Collection Number: *4-2A;* CSL Roll Number: *138;* FHL Roll Number: *978595* : accessed 27 Sept 2021).

[3] *The Times Picayune*, New Orleans, Louisiana, 20 Dec 1844, p. 3. (http://newspapers.com : accessed 4 Oct 2021).

[4] M. Mark Stolarik, ed. *Forgotten Doors: The Other Ports of Entry to the United States*, Chapter 3, "Immigration through the Port of New Orleans," by Joseph Logsdon (Philadelphia, Pa.: The Balch Institute Press, 1988.)

[5] Smithsonian Natural History Museum, *On The Water*, https://americanhistory.si.edu/onthewater : accessed 30 Aug 2021

[6] National Museums of Liverpool, Emigration to USA and Canada: Information sheet 12, Archives Centre, Maritime Museum, (https://www.liverpoolmuseums.org.uk/archivesheet13 : accessed 27 Sept 2021).

[7] M. Mark Stolarik, ed. *Forgotten Doors: The Other Ports of Entry to the United States*, Chapter 3, "Immigration through the Port of New Orleans," by Joseph Logsdon (Philadelphia, Pa.: The Balch Institute Press, 1988.)

[8] William Metcalfe, *A History of the County of Renfrew,* (1905) (http://electricscotland.com/history/renfrew : accessed 12 May 2022).

[9] William Metcalfe, *A History of the County of Renfrew* (1905) https://www.electricscotland.com/history/renfrew/ : accessed 27 Sept 2021.

---

¹⁰ 1860 U.S. Census, New Orleans, Louisiana, population schedule, Alice Waugh, image, Ancestry.com (http://ancestry.com : accessed 22 May 2022, citing NARA microfilm publication M653.

¹¹ New Orleans, Louisiana Death Records Index, 1804-1949, Alice McNichol Waugh, 27 April 1902 (http://ancestry.com : accessed 13 May 2022).

¹² U.S. Presbyterian Church Records, 1701-1709, New Orleans, Louisiana, Robert Waugh (http://ancestry.com : accessed 13 May 2022).

¹³ *The Times Picauyne*, New Orleans, 20 Dec 1844, p. 2.

¹⁴ *The Times-Picayune*, New Orleans, 20 Dec 1844, p. 1.

¹⁵ Passenger and Immigration Lists, 1500s-1900, Missouri, 1848, Page 43, Ancestry.com (http://ancestry.com : accessed 28 Sept 2021).

¹⁶ California State Library, Sacramento, California; Great Registers, 1868-1898 for James George Nicol, Collection No. 4-2A, CSL roll number 138, Ancestry.com (http://ancestry.com : accessed 28 Sept 2021).

¹⁷ 1850 U.S. Census, Madison, Illinois, population schedule, p. 429, James George McNicol, image, Anecestry.com (http://ancestry.com : accessed 18 April 2022), citing NARA microfilm publication M119.

¹⁸ 1850 U.S. Census, Madison, Illinois.

¹⁹ *Alton Telegraph & Review*, Oct 13, 1848, p. 2. (http://newspapers.com : accessed 8 Oct 2021).

²⁰ *Centennial History of Madison County, Illinois and Its People, 1812 to 1912*, Wilbur Norton, The Lewis Publishing Company, Chicago and New York, (1912)

²¹ *The Times Picayune*, p. 3. (http:// newspapers.com : accessed 8 Oct. 2021).

²² Lawrence Nicol, interview by Susan Nicol, Walnut Creek, CA, May, 1974, transcript privately held by Susan Nicol Thibodeaux, Tucson, AZ.

²³ 1860 U.S. Census, St. Bernard Parish, Louisiana, population schedule, p. 366, Dwelling No. 49, Colin McNicol, image, Ancestry.com (http://ancestry.com : accessed 2 Oct 2021), citing NARA microfilm publication M653.

²⁴ Scotland, Select Marriages, 1561-1910, Colin McNicol and Alice George, 1814, database with images, Ancestry.com (http://ancestry.com : accessed 2 Oct 2021).

²⁵ Scotland Select Marriages, 1561-1910, Archibald McNicol and Agnes Campbell, 1786, database with images, Ancestry.com (http://ancestry.com : accessed 2 Oct 2021).

²⁶ Encyclopedia Britannica, *The Highlands of Scotland*, (https://www.britannica.com/place/Scotland/The-Industrial-Revolution : accessed 3 Oct 2021).

²⁷ Clan Campbell Society, (ccsna.org/clan/Campbell history: accessed 3 Sept 2021) .

---

Chapter 2

[1] Edna Bryan Buckbee, *The Sage of Old Tuolumne*, 1935, New York, The Press of the Pioneers, Inc., p. 139.

[2] Buckbee, *The Saga of Old Tuolumne*, p. 89.

[3] Buckbee, *The Sage of Old Tuolumne*, p. 96.

[4] U.S. Find A Grave Index, 1600s-Current, James G. Nicol, b. Apr 1852, Tuolumne County, CA, D. Columbia, Tuolumne County.

[5] U.S. Find A Grave Index, 1600s-current, Francis David Nicol, b. 17 Feb 1859, d. 10 Mar 1910 (http://ancestry.com : accessed 12 May 2022).

[6] *Alton Weekly Courier*, "Conflict of the Century," 17 Feb 1859, p. 4. (http: newspapers.com : accessed 8 Oct 2021).

[7] Buckbee, *The Sage of Old Tuolumne*, p. 289.

[8] Tuolumne County, California, *The People of California against Patrick Flanigan*, January 1860, Tuolumne County Historical Society, Sonora, CA.

[9] Frank Coates, "The Early History of Tuolumne County, California," *Stockton Times*, 30 March 1850, p. 76.

[10] Buckbee, *The Sage of Old Tuolumne*, p. 124.

[11] 1860 U.S. Census, Tuolumne County, California, population schedule, p. 292, Dwelling 1796, James George Nicol, image, Ancestry.com (http://ancestry.com : accessed 4 Oct 2021), citing NARA microfilm publication M653.

[12] Deed from A. Lewis to James Nicol, Tuolumne County, 14 Oct. 1864, Vol. 13, P. 503-405. (Copy in Nicol Archives, Tucson, AZ).

[13] 1880 U.S. Census, Tuolumne County, California, population schedule, p. 163, Dwelling 31, James George Nicol, image Ancestry.com (http://ancestry.com : accessed 4 Oct 2021), citing NARA microfilm publication Roll 85.

[14] "Sad Bereavement of Attorney Frank D. Nicol", *The Evening Mail*, Stockton, CA, 9 June 1900, p. 7 (http://newspapers.com : accessed 20 Mar 2022).

Chapter 3

[1] I.E. Jones, Eulogy to Frank David Nicol, *Stockton Evening Standard*, 4 April 1910, archived edition, (http://newspapers.com : accessed 9 Oct 2021).

[2] "Setting the Standard Since 187," UC Hastings Law, San Francisco (http://uchastings.educ/our-story)

[3] "Closing Events of the Convention," *The Evening Mail*, p. 5, Stockton, CA, 03 Sept 1900, Frank D. Nicol (http//newspapers.com : accessed 8 April 2022).

[4] "Nicol's Position," *The Evening Mail*, 23 Aug 1900, Stockton, CA (http://newspapers.com : accessed 8 April 2022).

---

5 Jones, Eulogy to Frank David Nicol.

6 Memoriam to Frank D. Nicol, Calaveras County, Judge A.J. McSorley, 4 April 1910 (original document held by Nicol Family).

7 Tuolumne County, California, marriage license (1883), Frank David Nicol and Adelaide Dodge, Tuolumne County Historical Society, image, Ancestry.com (http://ancestry.com : accessed 10 Oct 2021).

8 U.S. World War I Draft Registration Cards, Queens, New York, Edwin Estel Nicol, 1918, Ancestry.com (http://ancestry.com : accessed 29 Dec 2021) citing NARA microfilm roll M1509.

9 "Literary Exercises on the Fourth," *The Evening Mail*, 21 June 1901, Stockton, CA (http://newspapers.com : accessed 8 April 2022).

10 "Society," *Stockton Evening Mail*, 23 May 1908, p. 4, Susan Nicol (http://newspapers.com : accessed 8 April 2022).

11 "Susan Nicol Smith Dies in San Mateo,: *San Francisco Chronicle*, 3 Jan 1959 (http://newspapers.com : accessed 8 April 2022).

12 "Miss Nicol Weds Lieut. Nielson of U.S. Navy," *The San Francisco Examiner*, 6 March 1914, p. 9 (http://newspapers.com : accessed 22 May 2022).

13 "United States Occupation of Veracruz," *Britannica*, 14 April 2022, (http://britannica.com/event/United-States-occupation-of-Veracruz : accessed 22 May 2022).

14 Nielson, Lieutenant Commander Joseph L. Papers, *Naval History and Heritage Command,* (http://history.navy.mil. : accessed 22 May 2022).

15 U.S. Select Military Registers, 1862-1985 for Joseph L. Nielson, File No. 7654 (http://ancestry.com : accessed 23 May 2022).

16 "Columnist's Sister Dies," *The San Francisco Examiner*, 16 March 1957, p. 35 (http://newspapers.com : accessed 29 Dec 2021).

17 Lawrence Nicol, interview, May, 1974,

18 "Judge Nicol of Tuolumne County Tries His Last Case", *Stockton Daily Evening Record*, 4 Dec 1922, p. 2. (http://newspapers.com : accessed 10 Oct 2021).

Chapter 4

1 "Sells Brothers Enormous United Shows," *The Mail,* 15 September 1888, p. 5 (http://newspapers.com/image/609790242).

2 Lawrence Nicol, interview, May, 1974.

3 Lawrence Nicol interview, May 1974.

4 U.S. School Yearbooks, 1880-2012, University of California, 1912 (http://ancestry.com : accessed 12 Oct 2021).

5 California Voter Registration List, 1900-1968, Lawrence Nicol, 1912, Democrat (http://ancestry.com : accessed 12 Oct 2021).

6 "Lawrence Nicol Honored," *The Evening Mail,* Stockton, California, p. 6 (http://newspapers.com : accessed 12 Oct 2021).

7 California Occupational Licenses, Registers, and Directories, 1876-1969, Lawrence Nicol, attorney, 14 May 1914 (http://ancestry.com : accessed 12 Oct 2021).

8 U.S., World War I Draft Registration Cards, San Francisco, Lawrence Nicol, 5 June 1917, Draft Card N, Ancestry.com (http://ancestry.com : accessed 11 Oct 2021) citing NARA microfilm roll M1509.

9 U.S. Army Honorable Discharge, #397591, Lawrence Nicol, Service Number 2278529, 22 July 1919, copy of original held by John T. Young, Tucson, AZ.

10 "Lawrence Nicol With Army At Camp Lewis," *Stockton Daily Evening Record,* Stockton, California, p. 3 (http://newspapers.com : accessed 11 Oct 2021).

11 Library of Congress, "The American Expeditionary Forces,", *Stars and Stripes,* (https://crsreports.congress.gov/product/pdf/RL/RL32492) : accessed 13 Oct 2021.

12 U.S. Army Transport Service Arriving and Departing Passenger Lists, 1910-1939, New York, Lawrence Nicol, 16 March 1918, image, Ancestry.com (http://ancestry.com : accessed 12 Oct 2021), citing NARA, Record Group 92, Roll 403.

13 U.S. Army Transport Service Arriving and Departing Passenger Lists, 1910-1939, Hoboken, New Jersey, Lawrence Nicol, 13 July 1919, image, Ancestry.com (http://ancestry.com : accessed 12 Oct 2021, citing NARA Record Group 92, Roll 125.

14 James L. Gilbert, *World War I and the Origins of U.S. Intelligence,* Scarecrow Press, Lanham, MD, 2012, p. 58.

15 Irene Hund, Marin County, California, interview by Jean Elliott Nicol, 15 June 1980, transcript privately held by Susan Nicol Thibodeaux, Tucson, AZ.

16 U.S. Army WWI Transport Service, Passenger Lists, 1910-1939, New York, Walter Hund, 11 Jan 1918, image, Fold3.com (http://Fold3.com : accessed 13 Oct 2021), citing NARA Record 620635190, p. 191.

17 Susan Nicol Thibodeaux and Todd Nicol, Board's Crossing, California, interview by John T. Young, 28 Sept 2020, transcript privately held by interviewer, Tucson, AZ.

18 Walter J. Hund, 58, Oil Chemist, Dies, *Oakland Tribune,* 18 Feb 1947, p. 15 (http://newspapers.com : accessed 13 Oct 2021).

19 Lawrence Nicol in Paris, *Stockton Daily Evening Record,* 29 May 1919, p. 4 (http://newspapers.com : accessed 13 Oct 2021).

20 Irene Hund, interview by Jean Elliott Nicol, 15 June 1980.

21 Lawrence Nicol, interview by Susan Nicol, May 1974.

22 Betsy Wing, "She stays where the action is" *Contra Costa Times,* 15 June 1987, p. 6A, Irene Hund Nicol. (copy of article in Nicol Archives, Tucson, AZ).

---

23 California Marriage Records from Select Counties, 1850-1941, Marin County, Lawrence Nicol and Irene Hund, 20 Dec 1920 (http://ancestry.com : accessed 13 Oct 2021).

24 1920 U.S. Census, population schedule, San Francisco, Enumeration District 154, Lawrence Nicol, image, Ancestry.com (http://ancestry.com : accessed 13 Oct 2021), citing NARA microfilm roll T625.

25 Lawrence Nicol, interview by Susan Nicol, May 1974.

26 "Irene Hund Weds," *San Francisco Examiner*, 26 Dec 1920, p. 73 (http://newspapers.com : accessed 13 Oct 2021).

27 1940 U.S. Census, population schedule, Contra Costa County, Enumeration District 7-48, Lawrence Nicol, image, Ancestry.com (http://ancestry.com : accessed 18 Oct 2021), citing NARA microfilm roll T627, p. 19B.

28 Lawrence Nicol, interview by Susan Nicol, May 1974.

29 Frank Nicol, interview by Susan Nicol, May 1974.

30 U.S. World War II Draft Cards, Berkeley, California, Walter Harry Nicol, 30 June 1942, image, Ancestry.com (http://ancestry.com :accessed 18 Oct 2021), NARA, St. Louis, Missouri, Record Group 147, Box 1314.

31 Garrett Nicol, Freestone, California, interview by John T. Young, 18 June 2021, transcript privately held by interviewer, Tucson, AZ.

32 Miss Jean Nicol Reveals Troth, *Oakland Tribune*, 12 May 1943, p. 12, (http://newspapers.com : accessed 18 Oct 2021).

33 Susan Nicol Thibodeaux and Todd Nicol interview, 2021.

Chapter 5

1 *The Bay of San Francisco, a history*, 1892, Lewis P:ublishing Co., Chicago, Vol. II.

2 New York Passenger Lists, 1820-1957, Frederick J. Hund, 1872, image, Ancestry.com (http://ancestry.com : accessed 30 Dec 2021) citing NARA microfilm roll 359.

3 New York Passenger Lists, 1820-1957, Maria and Sophia Hund, 1874, image, Ancestry.com (http://Ancestry.com : accessed 5 Jan 2022) citing NARA microfilm M237, Line 17.

4 New York Extracted Marriage Index, 1866-1937, database, entry for Maria Hund and Charles Hartung, 24 Jan 1978, Ancestry.com (http://ancestry.com : accessed 5 Jan 2022).

5 New Jersey Deaths and Burials Index, 1798-1971, Franklin, Bergen, New Jersey, Sophie Hund, 29 Oct 1896, Ancestry.com (http://ancestry.com : accessed 5 Jan 2022).

6 "Distinguished Men of the Time," *The San Francisco Call*, 03 Jan 1892, p. 2 (http://newspapers.com).

7 *The San Francisco Call*, 03 Jan 1892, p. 2.

8 California Voter Registers, 1866-1898, San Francisco, Frederick John Hund, Ancestry.com (http://ancestry.com : accessed 6 Jan 2022).

9 1900 U.S. Census, population schedule, Marin County; enumeration District 56, Frederick Hund, image, Ancestry.com (http://ancestry.com : accessed 6 Jan 2022), citing NARA Roll T623, p. 6A.

10 "San Francisco Earthquake, 1906," The Center for Legislative Affairs, (http://archives.gov/legislative/features/sf : accessed 6 Jan 2022).

11 Irene Hund Nicol, interview with Jean Elliott Nicol, 15 June 1980, Freestone, California. Transcript held by John T. Young, Tucson, AZ.

12 Irene Hund Nicol, interview, 1980.

13 "El Recreo Sanitarium," *Anne T. Kent California Room*, Jocelyn Moss, 27 Aug 2020 (http://annetkent.kontribune.com : accessed 6 Jan 2022).

14 Irene Hund Nicol, interview, 1980.

15 "Pioneers of Marin Hurt in Auto Crash," *San Anselmo Herald*, 22 June 1928, p. 1, (http://newspapers.com : accessed 6 Jan 2022).

16 "Death Calls to Dr. F.J. Hund," *San Anselmo Herald*, 22 May 1941, p. 8 http://newspapers.com : accessed 7 Jan 2022).

17 U.S. Naturalization Record Indexes, 17901-1992, San Francisco, Jacob Zech, 5 Nov 1860 (http://ancestry.com : accessed 07 Aug 2022).

18 Germany, Select Births and Baptisms, 1558-1898, Susanna Grass, 25 April 1831 (http://ancestry.com : accessed 07 August 2022).

19 "San Francisco in 1856", The Museum of the City of San Francisco, (http://sfmuseum.oprg/hist1/56hist.html : accessed 7 Jan 2022).

20 "San Francisco", *San Francisco Chronicle*, 03 Jan 1897, p. 15, (http://newspapers.com : accessed 7 Jan 2022).

21 "Jacob Zech, Piano-Forte Manufacturer," *San Francisco Chronicle*, 05 Sept 1865, p. 2, (hjttp://newspapers.com : accessed 7 Jan 2022).

22 Pacific Coast Directory, 1867, Jacob Zech, 416 Market, San Francisco, Ancestry.com. (http://ancestry.com : accessed 7 Jan 2022).

Chapter 6

1 California Department of Public Health, Birth Certificate, 1921, Frank David Nicol, Marin County Office of Vital Statistics.

2 Susan Nicol Thibodeaux, Board's Crossing interview, 2021.

3 Susan Nicol Thibodeaux, Board's Crossing interview, 2021.

4 Frank Nicol, interview by Susan Nicol, May 1974.

5 Marsh Maslin, "Among Those Who Danced 'Til Dawn," *San Francisco Call-Bulletin*, 13 April 1953.

6 California Marriage Index, Orange County, 7 Feb 1954, Frank D. Nicol and Jean K. Elliott, image, Ancestry.com (http://ancestry.com : accessed 15 Jan 2022.

7 Susan Nicol Thibodeaux, interview with John Young, 10 March 2022, Tucson, AZ.

[8] Frank Nicol, letter to family, 30 Dec 1961, 871 Moana Drive, San Diego. (Original held by Susan Nicol Thibodeaux in Tucson, AZ).

Chapter 7

[1] Todd Nicol, Board's Crossing interview. 2021.

[2] "Mountain Retreat Near Big Trees," *The Evening Mail*, 03 June 1907, p. 5, Frank D. Nicol (http://newspapers.com : accessed 8 April 2022).

[3] Judith Marvin, "East of Dorrington" (http:// CalaverasHistory.org : accessed 8 April 2022).

[4] California Death Index, 1905-1939, San Joaquin, Frank Nicol, 19 Mar 1910, image, Ancestry.com (http://ancestry.com : accessed 15 Jan 2022).

[5] "Nicol Children Lose Race Against Death," *San Francisco Call*, 21 Mar 1910, Frank D. Nicol (http://newspapers.com : accessed 23 July 2022).

[6] Washington, D.C. Marriage Records, 1810-1953, Francis Nicol Smith and Moira Archbold, 2 June 1938, Ancestry.com (http://ancestry.com : accessed 15 Jan 2022).

[7] Sharon Karr, *Traveler of the Crossroads*, Dorrington, CA, Log Cabin Manuscripts, 1994, p. 197.

[8] "Moira Archbold Selects June 2 For Her Wedding to Nicol Smith," *The San Francisco Examiner*, 05 May 1938, p. 15. (http://newspapers.com : accessed 15 Jan 2022).

[9] U.S. World War II Draft Cards, 1940-1947, Francis Nicol Smith, 16 Oct 1940, Ancestry.com (http://ancestry.com : accessed 22 Jan 2022), NARA, Records of the Selective Service, 147, Box 1684.

[10] "Capt. Nicol Smith Finds Japs Equaled by Jungle Leeches," *The San Francisco Examiner*, 29 Aug 1943, (http://newspapers.com : accessed 15 Jan 2022).

[11] "Nicol Smith in Tribute to Army Medical Force," *The San Francisco Examiner*, 5 Sept 1943, (http://newspapers.com : accessed 15 Jan 2022.

[12] Nicol Smith papers, Hoover Institution, Stanford University, Box 8, Folder CBI Daily Logs, Reproduced from National Archives, 1943.

[13] "Susan Nicol Smith," *The San Francisco Examiner*, 3 Jan 1959, (http://newspapers.com : accessed 20 Jan 2022).

[14] Telephone interview with Alan Nicol, June 2022.

[15] Frank Nicol letter to his family, 12 July 2005 (original held in Nicol archives, Tucson, AZ).

[16] Frank Nicol letter to his family, 20 Sept 2005. (original held in Nicol archives, Tucson, AZ).

[17] Frank Nicol letter to his family, 20 July 2005. (original held in Nicol archives, Tucson, AZ).

[18] Frank Nicol letter to his family, 25 Sept 2006 (original held in Nicol archives, Tucson, AZ).

19 Frank Nicol letter to his family, 13 Sept. 2007 (original held in Nicol archives, Tucson, AZ).

20 "San Franciscaena", *San Francisco Chronicle*, 5 Jan 1995, Herb Caen, (copy of article in author's possession).

Chapter 8

1 North American, Family Histories, 1500-2000, Adelaide Louise Dodge and Francis David Nicol, 30 Jul 1883, (http://ancestry.com : accessed 20 Jan 2022).

2 1880 U.S. Census, population schedule, San Francisco, Enumeration District 176, Adelaide Dodge, image, Ancerstry.com (http:ancestry.com : accessed 20 Jan 2022), citing NARA roll 78, p. 395B.

3 Western States Marriage Index, 1809-2011, Tuolumne County, California, 25 March 1855, Mark T. Dodge and Eliza L. Rodgers.

4 Rasmussen, Louis, San Francisco Ship Passenger Lists, Vol. 4, Genealogical Publishing Co., 2003, J.W. Dodge (http://ancestry.com : accessed 22 May 2022).

5 U.S. Find A Grave Index, 1600s-Current, New York, Jonathan Washington Dodge, d. Apr 1860 (http://ancestry.com : accessed 22 May 2022).

6 Caroline Adelaide Dodge, letter to Mark Dodge, 2 August 1862, (copy in Nicol Archives, Tucson, AZ).

7 Howard C. Gardiner, *In Pursuit of the Golden Dream*, Western Hemisphere Publishing Co, 1970, p. 225.

8 U.S. Revolutionary War Rolls, 1775-1783, Daniel Dodge, Ancestry.com (http://ancestry.com : accessed 23 Jan 2022), citing NARA microfilm M246, Record Group 93.

9 Passenger and Immigration Lists Index, 1500s-1900s, Rhode Island, Tristram Dodge, 1661, Ancestry.com (http://ancestry.com : accessed 23 Jan 2022).

10 1870 U.S. Census, San Francisco, California, population schedule, Ward 11, Nelson Rogers, (http://ancestry.com : accessed 7 August 2022), citing NARA roll M593.

11 1880 U.S. Census, Tuolumne County, California, population schedule, Enumeration District 107, Washington Dodge, (http://ancestry.com : accessed 23 Jan 2022), citing NARA Roll 85, p. 141D.

12 "Washington Dodge," *Encyclopedia Titanic*, (http://encyclopedia-titanica.org/titanic-survivor/washington-dodge.html. : accessed 23 Jan 2022).

13 "Mind of S.F. Leader Fails, Shoots Self," *The San Francisco Examiner*, 22 Jun 1919, p. 1, Dr. Washington Dodge, (http://newspapers.com : accessed 23 Jan 2022).

---

¹⁴ "Titanic Survivors Describe Awful Scene," *The Bulletin*, San Francisco, 19 April 1912 (http://sfmuseum.net/hist5/dodge.html)

[15] "Titanic Survivors Describe Awful Scene, *The Bulletin*.

[16] "The Dodge Family Are Home Again," *The Californian*, 01 May 1912, p. 3, (http://newspapers.com : accessed 22 Jan 2022).

[17] "Dr. Washington Dodge Speech on Titanic at Commonwealth Club," *San Francisco Chronicle*, 12 May 1912, San Francisco Museum, (http://www.sfmuseum.org/hist5/dodge6.html : accessed 22 Jan 2022).

[18] Titanic Inquiry Project, United States Senate Inquiry, Day 9, 27 April 1912 (http://titanicinquiry.org) : accessed 5 April 2022.

[19] Dodge, Titanic, Commonwealth Club.

[20] Dodge, Titanic, Commonwealth Club.

[21] Walter Lord, *A Night To Remember*, Henry Holt and Company, New York, p. 132.

[22] "Journal of Proceedings, Board of Supervisors," The Recorder, p. 7, 01 Aug.1912, San Francisco (http://newspapers.com : accessed 21 March 2022).

[23] West Point Inn, (http://westpointinn.com/history) : accessed 20 March 2022.

[24] "Mind of S.F. Leader Fails, Shoots Self," *The San Francisco Examiner*.

[25] " Bride's Letter From Jamestown, 1854," *Chispa, Quarterly of the Tuolumne County Historical Society*, Sonora, California, Vol. 15, No. 1, July-Sept 1975.

[26] Lawrence Nicol, interviewed by Susan Nicol, May 1974.

[27] 1850 U.S. Census, population schedule, Newbury, Orange, Vermont, Eliza Rogers, Ancestry.com (http://ancestry.comn : accessed 24 Jan 2022), citing NARA microfilm M432, Roll 926, p. 117a.

[28] "Obituary for Josiah Rogers," *East Barre Record*, 21 Jul 1898, p. 2, (http://newspapers.com : accessed 26 Jan 2022).

[29] Lawrence Nicol, interview with Susan Nicol, May 1974.

[30] B.F. Alley, *The History of Tuolumne County, California*, B.F. Alley, 1882, p. 244.

[31] "A Leading Mason Dead," *Los Angeles Times*, 30 Jun 1898, E.A. Rogers, (http://newspapers.com : accessed 26 Jan 2022).

[32] Letter to Jean Nicol from the Masons, 3 Apr 1978, copy of original held by John T. Young, Tucson, AZ.

[33] U.S. Revolutionary War Rolls, 1775-1783, New Hampshire militia, Josiah Rogers, (http://ancestry.com : accessed 26 Jan 2022), citing NARA microfilm M246, Record Group 93.

[34] Massachusetts Town Vital Collections, 1620-1988, Newbury, Massachusetts, Robert Rogers, 23 Dec 1663, (http://ancestry.com : accessed 26 Jan 2022).

Chapter 9

[1] California Birth Index 1905-1995, Los Angeles, 21 Dec 1923, Jean K. Elliott, (http://ancestry.com : accessed 27 Jan 2022).

[2] U.S. School Yearbooks, 1900-1999 for Jean Elliott, Long Beach, California, Polytechnic High School, 1941 (http://ancestry.com : accessed 27 Jan 2022)

[3] U.S. School Yearbooks, Polytechnic High School, Jean Elliott.

[4] "Jean Elliott, Frank Nicol Wed," *The San Francisco Examiner*, 08 Feb 1943, p. 33 (http://newspapers.com : accessed 31 Jan 2022).

[5] Thibodeaux, Susan Nicol, Interview, 10 March 2022.

[6] Frank Nicol letter to Genworth Financial, 4 Nov 2009 (original in Nicol Archives, Tucson, AZ).

[7] "Honeymoon in the Desert," *Star News*, 1 Dec 1960, p. 18, John Elliott and Emily Jones Hoyt (http://newspapers.com : accessed 2 Feb 2022).

Chapter 10

[1] Ohio, Births and Christenings Index, 1800-1962, Rose, Carroll, Ohio, Raymond Elliott, 9 Apr 1886 (http://ancestry.com : accessed 3 Feb 2022).

[2] 1980 letter from Esther Elliott Whitmer to Jean Elliott Nicol. Letter held in private possession of Susan Nicol Thibodeaux, Tucson, AZ.

[3] Cornell-Chicago Game Souvenir, Marshall Field, 14 Nov 1907 (original souvenir held by Kent Elliott in Newport Beach, CA).

[4] "Stagg Declares Maroons Outplayed Cornell Team," *The Inter Ocean*, Chicago, Ill., 16 Nov 1908, p. 9 (http://newspapers.com : accessed 14 April 2022).

[5] "Coach Stagg, Chicago," *Chicago Tribune*, 15 Nov 1908, p. 16 (http://newspapers.com : accessed 14 April 2022).

[6] "Coach Elliott From Long Beach Is Winning Fame," Press-Telegram, Long Beach, CA, 23 Nov 1916, p. 5 (http://newspapers.com : accessed 14 April 2022).

[7] "Civic Leader Pat Elliott Dead at 84," *The Orange County Evening News*, 19 Feb 1971, Raymond :Pat: Elliott.

[8] "Coach Elliott From Long Beach is Winning Fame," *Long Beach Press-Telegram*, 23 Nov 1916, p. 5, Raymond D. Elliott.

[9] U.S. World War I Draft Registration Cards, 1917-1918, Los Angeles County, Raymond Davis Elliott, (http://ancestry.com : accessed 4 Feb 2022), citing NARA microfilm roll 1531195.

[10] "Men's Chorus Holds Place in the Community," *The Whittier News*, Whittier, CA, 01 Jan 1921, p. 68. (http://newspapers.com : accessed 11 April 2022).

---

11 "Miss Mabel Marie Simpkins is Bride of Hal Will Smith," *The Whittier News,* Whittier, CA, 16 Jun 1925, p. 3 (http://newspapers.com : accessed 11 April 2022).

12 1910 U.S. Census, population schedule, Hunt County, Texas, District 0112, Mary Lou Sherrill, (http://ancestry.com : accessed 4 Feb 2022), citing NARA microfilm roll T624_1566, p. 7A.

13 U.S. School Yearbooks 1900-1999, North Texas State Normal College, Denton, 1907, Mary Lou Sherrill (http://ancestry.com : accessed 4 Feb 2022).

14 1920 U.S. Census, population schedule, Los Angeles County, District 207, Mary Lou Sherrill (http://ancestry.com : accessed 04 Feb 2022), citing NARA microfilm roll T625, p. 11B.

15 World War I Draft Registration Cards, 1917-1918, James Dudley Sherrill, Los Angeles (http://ancestry.com : accessed 6 May 2022).

16 U.S. Veterans Administration Master Index, 1917-1940, James Dudley Sherrill, San Diego, July 1920 (http://ancestry.com : accessed 6 Mayr 2022).

17 "Nominees Confirmed for Planning Unit, Harbor Commission," *Long Beach Press-Telegram,* Raymond D. Elliott, 19 Jul 1949, p. 15,.

18 "Summer Study for Air Raid, Fire Wardens," *The Long Beach Sun,* 16 May 1942, p. 3. (http://newspapers.com : accessed 10 April 2022).

19 *The Orange County Evening News,* 19 Feb 1971.

20 1900 U.S. Census, population schedule, District 43, Carroll County, Ohio, John M. Elliott (http://ancestry.com : accessed 16 Feb 2022), citing NARA microfilm 1241244.

21 1870 U.S. Census, population schedule, Rose, Carroll County, Ohio, James Elliott (http://ancestry.com : accessed 16 Feb 2022), citing NARA microfilm roll M593.

22 Carroll County, Ohio, Veteran Grave Registrations, 1817-1980, James B. Elliott, Rose Township, Ohio (http://ancestry.com : 16 Feb 2022).

23 U.S. Find A Grave Index, 1600s-current, Aaron I. Elliott, Monroe Township, Carroll County, Ohio (http://ancestry.com : accessed 6 May 2022).

24 U.S. Find A Grave Index, 1600s-Current, Carroll County, Ohio, George M. Elliott, b. 4 March 1822, d. 28 Feb 1870, (http://ancestry.com : accessed 17 April 2022).

25 Ohio, U.S. Tax Records, 18900-1850 Carroll County, Aaron Elliott, Reference ID 173 (http://ancestry.com : accessed 16 Feb 2022).

26 Passenger and Immigration Lists Index, 1500s-1900s, Aaron Elliott, Ohio (http://ancestry.com : accessed 24 July 2022).

Chapter 11

[1] *Handbook of Texas, Fannin County*, Texas State Historical Association, (http://tsaonline.org.handbook/entries/fannin-county : accessed 09 Feb 2022).

[2] Texas Death Certificates, 1903-1982, J.S. Sherrill, 15 Feb 1931 (http://ancestry.com : accessed 22 July 2022).

[3] "A Bit of Fannin County History," *Honey Grove Signal*, 24 Dec 1909 (http: //fannincountyhistory.org : accessed 09 Feb 2022).

[4] "Judge James S. Sherrill Dies at Houston Home," *Greenville Evening Banner*, 16 Feb 1931, p. 1 (http://newspapers.com : accessed 09 Feb 2022).

[5] "James Sherrill obit", *Greenville Evening Banner*, 16 Feb 1931, p. 1 (http://newspapers.com : accessed 10 Feb 2022).

[6] 1920 U.S. Census, population schedule, Houston Ward 4, Harris County, TX, James Sherrill, (http://ancestry.com : accessed 16 Feb 2022), citing NARA microfilm roll T625_1813, P. 14A.

[7] Tunica County, Archives of Mississippi, 1840-1844, Byrd Sherrill (http://ancestry.com : accessed 22 July 2022).

[8] 1850 U.S. Census, population schedule, Tunica County, Mississippi, Byrd Sherrill (http://ancestry.com : accessed 22 July 2022).

[9] Tennessee Census, 1810-91, Roane County, tax list, 1805, Jesse Sherrill (http://ancestry.com : accessed 21 Feb 2022).

Chapter 12

[1] Civil War Service Records, Confederate Officers, Quartermasters in the Trans-Mississippi Department, Capt. James Farr, 13 Feb 1865, (http://fold 3 : accessed 22 Feb 2022) citing NARA microfilm M331, Record Group 109, p. 2.

[2] 1850 U.S. Census, population schedule, Hickman, Kentucky, James Farr (http://ancestry.com : accessed 22 July 2022), citing NARA microfilm M432.

[3] 1860 U.S. Census, population schedule, Hunt County, Texas, James Farr (http://ancestry.com : accessed 22 Feb 2022), citing NARA microfilm M653.

[4] U.S. and International Marriage Records, 1560-1900, James Farr and Laurena Finney Stevens, 1859 (http://ancestry.com : accessed 22 July 2022).

[5] Texas State Historical Association, *Handbook of Texas*, 01 Jan 1995, Austin, Texas (https://www.tshaonline.org/handbook/entries/farr).